KU-710-500

The
Huge Joke
Book

Where to find more Clarion value

Clarion books are sold in huge volumes wherever the best books cost *far* less.

They can also be purchased from the comfort of your armchair. Please send to the address on the back of the title page opposite, a stamped, self-addressed envelope for our *free catalogue*; or just browse the Internet at **www.clarion-books.co.uk** to discover our wide range of informative bestsellers, subject by subject.

If you have been particularly pleased with any one title, do please mention this to your bookseller as personal recommendation helps us enormously.

The
Huge Joke
Book

With jokes contributed by

Kevin Goldstein-Jackson,
Ernest Ford and A C H Newman

Copyright notice

First published by *Clarion* MCMXCV.
Material in this book has been drawn from *Newman's Joke & Story Book, Select A Joke, British & Other Jokes, Joke After Joke, Right Joke For The Right Occasion, Jokes For Telling* and *Blackpool Laffs*. This edition published by arrangement with Elliot Right Way Books. © A C H Newman MCMLXIV, MCMLXX and MCMLXXIX, Ernest Ford MCMXCV and Elliot Right Way Books MCMLXXIII, MCMLXXVII and MCMLXXXVI.

All rights reserved. No part of this book may be reproduced, stored in a retrieval system, or transmitted, in any form or by any means, electronic, photocopying, mechanical, recording or otherwise, without the prior permission of the copyright owner.

Conditions of sale
This book shall only be sold, lent, or hired, for profit, trade or otherwise, in its original binding, except where special permission has been granted by the Publishers.

Whilst care is taken in selecting Authors who are authoritative in their subjects, it is emphasised that their books can reflect their knowledge only up to the time of writing. Information can be superseded and printers' errors can creep in. This book is sold, therefore, on the condition that neither Publisher nor Author can be held legally responsible for the consequences of any error or omission there may be.

Typeset in 11/12pt Times by County Typesetters, Margate, Kent.
Printed and bound in Great Britain by Cox & Wyman Ltd., Reading, Berkshire

Clarion: published from behind no. 80 Brighton Road, Tadworth, Surrey, England. For information about our company and the other books we publish, visit our web site at www.clarion-books.co.uk

Contents

ANIMALS

1. John: 'I have one of the most intelligent cats in the world.'

Simon: 'What does it do?'

John: 'Watch me pretend to shoot it. Bang! You're dead!'

Simon: 'But the cat didn't do anything – he's still just licking his paws.'

John: 'That's what I mean about him being intelligent: he knew he wasn't dead.'

2. Two students shared a flat and a cat. Neither of the students was a particularly good cook.

One day one of the students returned to find his flatmate wringing his hands in despair.

'What happened?' asked the student.

'The cat ate your dinner.'

'Don't worry,' replied the first student. 'We'll buy another cat tomorrow.'

3. The vet had just supervised the delivery of a litter of kittens to the old spinster's cat. 'I just don't know how it could have happened,' said the spinster. 'Tibbles is never allowed out and no other cats are ever allowed into the house.'

'But what about him?' asked the vet, pointing to a large tom cat sitting in an armchair.

'Oh, don't be silly,' replied the spinster. 'That's her brother.'

4. A tom cat owned by an elderly lady stayed out so

late at night that she decided to take him to the vet.

On his return, however, the cat still stayed out late so the old lady thought that she would follow him and find out where he went. Very cautiously she crept after him, down a back alley, into a yard, where, surrounded by an admiring ring of other 'toms', he was holding court.

And the moral of that story is: even if you have lost the where-withal, so long as you retain the know-how, you can always set up as a consultant.

5. I was up until 2:30 this morning. I had to wait for the cat to come in so that I could let it out!

6. The little old lady went to the taxidermist and took from her bag two large, but dead, cats.

'These poor creatures were mine,' she said. 'They were always so very much in love – Fred and Freda – and it almost broke my heart when they died. Can you stuff them in a lifelike manner?'

'Certainly, madam,' replied the taxidermist. 'Do you want them mounted?'

The little old lady thought for a moment, then shook her head sadly: 'I know they were very much in love, but I think it would be more – how shall I put it? – delicate, if they were just holding paws instead.'

7. A new cat, a handsome Tom, had come to the neighbourhood, and all the other cats were very interested so one of their number had the first date.

'Well,' they chorused the next morning, 'how did you get on?'

'Pooh,' replied the favoured creature, rather a nice Persian. 'An absolutely wasted evening, my dears. All he did was talk about his operation!'

8. A man dashed into a police station at midnight. 'My wife,' he gasped. 'Will you find my wife? She's been missing since eight this evening, I must find her.'

'Particulars?' asked the sergeant. 'Height, weight?'

'I don't know,' replied the man.

'Do you know how she was dressed?'

'No, but she took the dog with her.'

'What kind of dog?' asked the sergeant.

'Brindle, bull-terrier, weight 53lbs. Four dark blotches on his body shading from grey to white, three white legs and right front leg brindled all but the toes. A small nick in his left ear.'

'That'll do,' gasped the sergeant. 'We'll find the dog.'

9. 'That's a lovely bulldog you've got there.'

'No, it's not a bulldog – it was chasing a cat and ran into a wall.'

10. 'I've just lost my dog.'

'Why don't you put an advertisement in the paper?'

'Don't be silly – my dog can't read.'

11. Man: 'I took my dog to the vet today because it bit my wife.'

Friend: 'Did you have it put down?'

Man: 'No, of course not – I had its teeth sharpened.'

12. The two fleas were just leaving the theatre when the male flea turned to the female flea and said: 'Shall we walk, or take a dog?'

13. Henrietta: 'Whenever we go out we let our puppy stay at home to look after the children.'

Clara: 'Is that safe?'

Henrietta: 'Of course. It's a baby setter.'

14. Two dogs were walking along the pavement. Suddenly one dog stopped and said: 'My name is Bonzo. What's your name?'

The other dog scratched and thought for a bit, and then replied: 'Well, I think it's Get Down Boy.'

15. My boss is so wealthy he even bought a kid for his dog to play with.

16. Advert: Rottweiler for sale. Very fond of people. Reluctant to let go!

17. The young man knew his aged aunt was extremely wealthy and dearly loved her poodles, so he visited her every day to take the dogs for walks in the hope of convincing his aunt that he was a suitable major beneficiary under her will.

A short time later the old lady died. She left him the poodles.

18. Edward was walking through the park one afternoon when he heard a female voice cry out: 'Get down, you beast! If you put your filthy paws on me once more I'll never come on the grass again.'

He rushed behind the hedge towards the sound of the voice, hoping to rescue a fair maiden from a foul creep – but instead discovered a little old lady talking to her pet dog.

19. A man was visiting a colleague who had rather a ferocious looking dog which barked loudly at him as he walked up the path. So he said, 'My word, your dog does bark. I even thought he was going to bite me!'

His colleague replied, 'Oh, he's all right. You know the saying: "A barking dog never bites".'

'Yes,' said the first man, 'I know the saying, and you know the saying, but does the dog know it?'

20. Fred: 'We've got a new dog. Would you like to come and play with him?'

Tom: 'I've heard him barking and growling. He sounds very fierce and unfriendly. Does he bite?'

Fred: 'That's what I want to find out.'

21. Man: 'My dog has no tail.'
Friend: 'How do you know when it's happy?'
Man: 'When it stops biting me.'

22. A woman with a dog entered a shop and the shopkeeper noticed that the dog started to prowl about, so, becoming alarmed, he asked the woman: 'What do you call your dog?'
'Oh, we call him Carpenter,' she replied. 'You see, he's fond of doing little odd jobs about the house.'
'Well,' said the shopkeeper, 'if I put my boot behind him, do you think he might make a bolt for our door?'

23. A group of men were standing around talking and one had a dog with him.
'That's a fine dog,' said one of the men and his owner replied, 'He's a fine sporting dog, can smell out game a mile off.' He then noticed that the animal was sniffing around one of the men and said, 'That's funny, he can smell game now. Have you any on you or have you been carrying any in your pockets?'
'No,' replied the other man, then as though struck by a sudden inspiration, 'but my name's Partridge!'

24. In a dozey Western town a man was finding it rather difficult to get any sleep due to the howling and growling of his neighbour's dog which kept up a continuous racket all through the night. Feeling that enough was enough he decided to confront the owner and knocked vigorously at his door. The door opened and revealed a giant of a man wearing a dirty string vest. He was the nearest look alike to Desperate Dan it would be possible to get.
'Yep?' he said to the man.
'Is that your dog that barks all night?' he asked.
'Yep,' said the neighbour.
'Do you know that I can't get any sleep?' said the man.

'Yep,' he said, spitting a chew of tobacco past the man's ear.

'As I said, I can't get any sleep,' said the man nervously.

'Nope. And what do you aim to do about it?' the dog owner asked, pressing a gun to the man's forehead.

'I'll put it in *my* yard tonight and see how *you* like it,' he said.

25. It was one of the strangest looking dogs they had ever seen at the pub, and the regulars found it a great topic of conversation.

Eventually, one of them sidled over to the dog's owner and said: 'That's a stupid looking dog you've got there. Can it fight?'

'Sure,' replied the owner.

'Well,' said the man, 'I bet you £20 that my labrador can beat your dog.'

The owner accepted the bet and the labrador was led in to fight. After twenty-two seconds the labrador lay dead on the floor. The loser, looking down at his dead dog, shook his head sadly and said: 'Your dog can certainly fight. But I still think it's a funny looking dog.'

'Yes,' agreed the owner. 'And it looked even funnier until I shaved its mane off.'

26. A traveller in Africa was staying in a remote part of the country. One day as he left the veranda of his dwelling a lion leapt at him but he had the presence of mind to duck and the lion jumped over his head. This happened again a morning or so later with the lion clearing off into the bush after missing him. Being very cautious by now, the traveller next day looked through the window before venturing out. To his astonishment, there before the veranda, was the lion practising low jumps.

27. One day the lion woke up feeling better than he

had ever done before. He felt so fit and healthy, he could beat the world. So he rose proudly and went for a prowl in the jungle. Soon he came across a snake and the lion stopped.

'Who is the king of the jungle?' asked the lion.

'You, of course,' replied the snake, and slithered away.

Next the lion came to a small pool where he found a crocodile.

'Who is the king of the jungle?'

'Why, you are,' replied the crocodile and slid into the murky depths of the water.

This went on all morning, all the animals agreeing that the lion was king of the jungle. Then he came across an elephant.

'Who is king of the jungle?' asked the lion.

In reply, the elephant picked up the lion with its trunk, hurled the lion around in the air and then bashed him against the ground and stamped on him.

'All right, all right,' groaned the battered lion. 'There's no need to get angry just because you don't know the answer.'

28. Why are elephants grey? To distinguish them from blackberries.

29. An elephant sat down on a canary which rather naturally squeaked in protest, whereupon the elephant said with a sneer: 'So, you're yeller and can't take it!'

30. The only reason elephants never forget is because they have nothing to remember.

31. What is the largest species of mouse in the world? A hippopotamouse.

32. A baby mouse saw a bat for the first time in its life and ran home, screaming, to its mother saying it had just seen an angel.

33. The sun-scorched vampire was crawling through the desert, crying 'Blood! Blood!'

34. I've just buried a very unfortunate firefly. It met its death trying to make love to a cigarette end.

35. One day two male centipedes were standing in the street when a female centipede strolled past.

One male centipede turned to the other and said: 'Now, there goes a nice pair of legs, pair of legs, pair of legs, pair of legs, pair of legs . . .'

36. 'And I shall call that creature a rhinoceros,' said Adam, pointing to a rhinoceros.

'But why call it that?' asked Eve.

'Because,' snapped Adam, 'it looks like a rhinoceros – that's why, stupid!'

37. The philosophical goldfish swam around in his bowl, then stopped for a few seconds and turned to his companion and asked: 'Do you believe in the existence of God?'

'Yes,' replied the second goldfish. 'Who else do you suppose changes our water?'

38. My niece thought that a kipper was a fish that slept a lot.

39. 'Why haven't you changed the water in the goldfish bowl like I asked you to do?'

'Because they haven't drunk the first lot yet.'

40. What do you call a camel with three humps? Humphrey.

41. Husband: 'It says in this article that over 5,000 camels are used each year to make paint brushes.'

Wife: 'Isn't it amazing what they can teach animals to do nowadays!'

42. A camel decided to educate his son who he suspected was getting a little inquisitive.

'Why do we have two humps?' asked the son. 'That's so that we can go for days and weeks without water. We can store it in the humps.'

'Why do we have very long eye lashes?' 'That,' he was told, 'is to protect the eyes from the sand in a sand storm.'

'And why do we have bulbous looking feet?' 'That is so that we can travel twice as fast through the desert.'

'Dad,' asked the young camel, 'what the hell are we doing in this zoo?'

43. The mother kangaroo suddenly leapt into the air and gave a cry of pain and anguish.

'Sidney!' she screamed. 'How many more times do I have to tell you that you cannot smoke in bed!'

44. A little girl who was taken to a zoo tossed some pieces of bun to a stork which gobbled them greedily and looked to her for more.

'What bird is it, Mummy?' she asked. The mother replied that it was a stork. 'Ooooh!' the little girl cried as she opened her eyes with astonishment. 'It must have recognized me!'

45. For three years Amy Clegg's parrot had not said a single word, and eventually she became convinced it was simply a stupid parrot unable to learn to speak English.

Then one day, as she was feeding it a piece of lettuce as a special treat, the parrot suddenly squawked: 'There's a maggot on it; there's a maggot on it!'

Amy Clegg was astonished. 'You can talk!' she exclaimed. 'But why haven't you spoken in all the three years that I've been keeping you?'

'Oh,' replied the parrot, 'the food has been excellent up to now.'

46. Jim loved his elderly grandmother dearly and decided that for Christmas he would buy her a parrot as it would be someone for her to talk to and keep her company.

He went to a pet shop and insisted that the parrot had to have a large vocabulary and he ended up paying a thousand pounds for what the pet shop owner assured him was the most talkative parrot he'd ever seen.

Jim arranged for the parrot to be delivered to his grandmother on Christmas Eve and on Christmas Day he phoned her and asked: 'How did you like the bird I sent you?'

'It was delicious!' she replied.

47. Mrs Green had a truly remarkable parrot and when the vicar came to tea one afternoon she could not resist demonstrating to him how clever her pet was.

'If you pull this little string on its left leg, Polly will sing "Abide With Me",' said Mrs Green, proudly. 'And if you pull the string on its right leg it will sing "Onward Christian Soldiers".'

'How remarkable!' exclaimed the vicar. 'And what happens if you pull both strings at once?'

'Simple!' replied the parrot. 'I fall off my perch, you stupid old twit.'

48. Fred at last could see a way of making a fortune. He had trained his parrot, after months of hard work, to tell jokes. At last he felt ready to cash in on all his hard work, so he took the parrot down to his local pub.

'This is my incredible joke telling parrot,' boasted Fred.

'Go on,' jeered the pub regulars. 'We'll give you ten to one that your parrot can't tell us a joke.'

'All right,' replied Fred. 'I accept your bet.'

But try as he could, Fred was unable to make the parrot talk – let alone tell jokes.

Fred left the pub, dismally, having lost the bet. On the way home he shook the parrot and shouted: 'What do you mean by keeping quiet, you stupid bird? You made me lose a ten to one bet!'

'Ah!' squawked the parrot. 'Tomorrow you'll be able to get fifty to one.'

49. Two men were fitting a wall-to-wall carpet in an elderly lady's house when they noticed a bump right in the middle of the carpet. As they had finished fitting it, the workmen didn't really relish the thought of taking up the carpet again, especially as one of the workmen said: 'It must be that empty packet of cigarettes I was going to throw away.'

Thus, in order to get rid of the bump, the two workmen jumped up and down on it and it was soon flattened and the carpet now looked perfect.

Just then the lady came into the room and said: 'Excuse me, but I wondered if you had seen my budgie anywhere? It's hurt its wing and can't fly and so it just walks around on the floor.'

50. What do you call a budgie run over by a lawn mower?
Shredded tweet.

51. What do you call a nine foot budgie?
Sir.

52. Where does a nine foot budgie sleep?
Anywhere it wants to!

53. Why do birds fly south in winter? Because it's too far to walk.

54. A woodpecker was talking to a chicken. 'Woodpeckers are much cleverer than you chickens.'

'What makes you say that?' asked the chicken. 'You seem to spend all your day banging your head against a tree.'

'Ah!' responded the woodpecker. 'But have you ever heard of Kentucky Fried Woodpecker?'

55. When it is very stormy and pouring with rain owls are not very keen to go romancing. All they do is sit in the trees looking dejected – hence their call: 'Too wet to woo; too wet to woo.'

56. Speaking about the droppings of pigeons in the town, a council official said: 'We must try not to dodge the issue.'

57. The beaver said to the tree: 'It's good to gnaw you.'

58. How do porcupines make love? Carefully, very carefully.

59. How do you keep flies out of the kitchen? Put a bucket of manure in the lounge.

60. Then there were the two worms in the graveyard making love in dead Ernest.

61. The only reason bees buzz is because they can't whistle.

62. Two men were sitting on the bank of a river in Africa, dangling their feet in the water. Suddenly one let out a yell and the other said: 'What's the matter?'

The first man replied: 'A crocodile has just bitten off one of my feet!'

'Which one?' the other asked.

'What does it matter?' came the reply. 'Those crocodiles all look alike to me.'

63. What do you call a crocodile at the North Pole? Lost.

64. 'Did you hear about Adam?' asked the brown rat.
'No. What happened?' said the black rat.
'He was feeling rather depressed and flushed himself down the toilet.'
'Oh!' said the black rat. 'He committed sewercide.'

65. As the exhausted American rabbit said: 'Gee, I'll never do that for ten bucks again!'

66. Why does a giraffe have such a long neck? Because it can't stand the smell of its feet.

67. How do you stop moles digging in the garden? Hide all the shovels.

68. The box of mothballs I bought last week aren't very good. The house is still full of moths. Every time I throw a mothball at them they fly out of the way and I've only managed to hit one.

69. Down at the Farmers Arms the local farmers met to have a drink and discuss animal prices and the transactions that had taken place in the market pens. Obviously, talk drifted to other things and ended with the different ways that their cows had been served.
'Oye sticks wi' the old fashioned way,' boasted old Farmer Giles. 'It ain't ever let us down,' he went on.
A young man from agricultural college overheard the conversation and asked if they hadn't tried artificial insemination on some of their stock.
'I've never heard of it,' replied Farmer Giles, 'and how can you serve a cow without a bull being there?'

The young man thrust a card into his hand and suggested that if he was interested to ring the town vet as instructed.

Farmer Giles pondered over this all the way home and wondered just how a cow could be served without the use of a bull. Flinging the door open he reached for the telephone and rang the number printed on the card. 'Oy'm ringing about this insemination,' he told the vet. 'Oy wants my cow served as soon as you can.'

'All right,' said the vet. 'Wash the cow's hind quarters very thoroughly, put down some clean straw and have a bucket of hot water and a stool handy, then give me a ring as soon as it's done.'

The farmer busied himself straight away and when he was satisfied he picked up the phone and rang the vet.

'Have you washed its hind quarters and laid down some straw? Did you remember the bucket of water and a stool?' asked the vet.

'Oy've done all that,' answered the farmer, 'and oy've even knocked a nail in the door for you to hang your breeches on!'

70. Farmer: 'Stop it! Stop it! Why are you beating the feet of the cows like that and making them jump up and down?'

Brian: 'I'm trying to make a milk shake.'

71. An old lady was the owner of a small farm and prided herself on the neatness of everything, although she owned only a few animals. She was a bit concerned about her prize pig who had looked under the weather lately and thought that perhaps what she required was the attention of a male pig.

Passing the neighbouring farm on market day the old lady decided to call to ask if the farmer would allow his male pig to do the necessary. The farmer agreed and told her to bring her sow around the next day. Not owning any form of transport, the old lady decided to sit her pig in the wheelbarrow and push it to her neighbour's farm.

'Now just leave these two pigs alone for half an hour whilst we go in to have a cup of tea and I'm sure that the job will be done by the time we return. But if in another two days your pig seems as restless as before, bring her back and we'll give them the afternoon together.'

Two days passed and the pig again began to look restless, so out came the wheelbarrow and again the pig was pushed to the neighbouring farm. The same instructions were given by the farmer, until by the end of the week tread marks were noticeable along the country lane between the two farms.

'I'm sure that it must have taken by now,' thought the farmer, so he decided to give his neighbour a call. 'Does she still look listless?' he asked over the phone.

'I don't know,' said the old lady, 'because I can't see the field from here. Just hold the line whilst I nip upstairs and look through the bedroom window.'

A few minutes passed before the receiver was picked up again.

'Can you see her?' asked the farmer.

'Yes, yes,' he was told.

'And what is she doing?' he wanted to know.

'She's sat in the wheelbarrow,' said the old lady.

72. In view of all the adverse publicity given about pets and to show that he was indeed a thoughtful parent, Fred decided to talk to his son on the subject to illustrate that some pets, when given love, in return prove to be one of the family. This particular family's pet was a tortoise.

'Tommy, our tortoise, has been in our family since long before you were born,' he told his son.

'Will he always live?' asked his son.

'Not always,' was the reply, 'but when he dies, Tommy won't want us to be sad for him.'

'Can we have a party?' asked the enquiring mind.

'Of course we can,' said the father, 'and invite all your friends.'

'Dad . . .' the child nestled up to his father. 'Can I kill him now?'

73. A man brought his pet octopus into the pub and said that he'd trained it to play any musical instrument in the whole of Britain.

At first, the pub regulars jeered, but after they had witnessed the octopus play a flute, the violin and then a saxophone their scepticism turned into virtual amazement.

Even more difficult and complex instruments were called for – and the octopus could play them all: the harpsichord, tuba and bassoon.

Then someone produced some bagpipes and the octopus appeared delighted – and proceeded to jump on them but did not produce any music.

'Why aren't you making music?' asked the owner of the octopus.

'Make music?' queried the octopus. 'I thought I was supposed to make love with it.'

74. A professor dedicated his whole life to research on arachnids and their behaviour. Eventually, after many years of patient study, he was ready to announce his findings to the world.

A special meeting of the world's top experts on arachnids was arranged, and the meeting was thrown open to the press as well – for the professor felt his findings were so amazing that the whole world should be informed.

When the audience were all seated, the professor strode into the room, ready to reveal the result of his researches. He placed a spider on a table in front of him and commanded it to walk three paces forward. To the astonishment of the audience, the spider did as it was ordered.

'Now take three paces backwards,' commanded the professor. Again, the spider obeyed the command.

Then the professor pulled all the legs off the spider, put it back on the table and said: 'Walk forward three paces.' The spider did not move. 'Walk forward three paces,' commanded the professor again. But still the spider did not move.

'You see,' said the professor, proudly. 'That proves that when you pull its legs off it can't hear.'

75. Nan had always been a pet lover and when her budgie died she knew that she must replace it with another pet, if only to keep her sanity by having something to talk to. After tidying herself up she reached for her bus pass to make the journey to town where she intended to visit the pet shop. The shop came into view and after the ting of the bell she found herself inside the shop and confronted by the owner.

Nan told the owner of her predicament and, thinking of all the feathers and empty seed shells that she had had to hoover constantly, decided that some other type of pet might do. The owner came to her assistance and suggested that a hamster might be just what she needed and so Nan took his advice.

A nice little home was made for the hamster which seemed to take to its new surroundings but on the fifth day when Nan awoke she found the hamster dead. Hurriedly she dressed and caught the bus in to town to report this to the pet shop owner but as the hamster was in perfect health when it left the shop, there was little he could do about it.

'Some people I know,' said the owner, 'who have had the same problem, stuff the carcass into a jam jar, and when it ferments it has made perfect jam.'

Nan went home and stuffed the hamster's carcass into a large jam jar and left it for about a month.

Taking it down from the shelf she lifted the lid and tasted. The taste was horrid, so immediately she took it out into the garden and threw it onto the lawn. Within a week where the jam had been thrown there had grown a patch of daffodils.

Without wasting any time she again caught the bus and went around to the pet shop to tell its owner of the amazing discovery of the daffodils appearing where she had thrown the jam.

The owner looked amazed and eyed Nan with a quizzical look.

'Are you sure that they are daffodils?' he asked.

'Of course I am,' said Nan. 'Why?'

'Because,' said the owner, 'we usually get *tulips* from hamster jam.'

76. A friend of mine has just invented a wonderful new insecticide. You spray it on all your plants and it promptly kills them so that the insects will then starve to death.

77. I went to the local chemist and said: 'Have you any poison that will kill mice?'

He said: 'No, have you tried Boots?'

I said: 'I want to poison them, not kick 'em to death!'

78. One man was trying to sell another man a horse.

'Well,' said the latter, 'he looks a decent animal, but is he well bred?'

'Well bred?' said the first man. 'Do you know, that animal is so well bred that if he could talk, he wouldn't speak to either of us!'

79. The young man walked into the petshop and asked if he could buy 387 beetles, 18 rats and 5 mice.

'I'm sorry, sir, but we can only supply the mice. But what did you want all the other creatures for?' asked the petshop manager.

'I was thrown out of my flat this morning,' replied the young man. 'And my landlord says I must leave the place exactly as I found it.'

BOOKS

80. *How To Juggle With Empty Beer Bottles* by Beatrix

81. *How to Make An Igloo* by S K Mow

82. *Twenty-Six Letters In Order* by Alf A Bet

83. *How To Make Solid Meals* by C Ment

84. *Sleepless Nights Together* by Constance Norah

85. *Panties Fall Down* by Lucy Lastic

86. *No Food* by M T Cupboard

87. *Bull Fighting* by Mat A Dore

88. *How To Tame Lions* by Claude Bottom

89. *Horse Riding Competitions* by Jim Karna

90. *Highwaymen Throughout The Ages* by Stan Dan D Liver

91. *Pass The Sick Bags* by Eve Itt-Upp

92. *Home Haircutting* by Shaun Hedd

93. *How To Improve Your Memory* by Ivor Gott

94. *Not Quite The Truth* by Liza Lott

95. *Neck Exercises* by G Rarff

96. *The Naughty Boy* by U R A Payne

97. *The Art Of Striptease* by Eva Drawsoff

98. *Singing Between Tenor and Bass* by Barry Tone

99. *Uncertainty* by R U Shore

100. *Outsize Clothes* by L E Fant

101. *Deathly Cookery* by R Snick

102. *How To Grow Squashy Red Fruit* by Tom R Tow

103. *Carpet Fitting For All* by Walter Wall

104. *Very Old Furniture* by Anne Teak

105. *Procedures for Analysis of Reading Problems in Children at Key Stage 1* by Liz Dexia.

106. *Want A Kiss?* by Miss L Toh

107. *Do-It-Yourself Brain Surgery* by Drs Out & I Malone

108. *Lucky Numbers* by Lottie Reese

109. *A Treat For A Sly Cat* by Ken Airy

110. *Motorway Chaos* by Laurie Jack Nife

111. *Jamaican Steeples* by Belinda Belfry

112. *How To Win* by Vic Tree

113. *Court Witness* by Tel d'Truffe

BOSSES

114. My boss thinks very highly of me. Today he even called me a perfect nonentity!

115. Our boss is so popular everybody wants to work for him – the local undertaker, the gravedigger . . .

116. The only reason my boss never says an unkind remark about anyone is because he only ever talks about himself.

117. Employee: 'Sir, my wage packet this week was empty.'
Boss: 'I know. They don't make money in small enough denominations to pay you what you're worth.'

118. My boss is so unpopular even his own shadow refuses to follow him around.

119. You can't help admiring our boss. If you don't, you don't work here any more.

120. The managing director looked around the boardroom after making his speech in favour of a particular course of action.
'Now,' he said, 'we'll take a vote on my recommendations. All those in opposition raise your right arm and say "I resign".'

121. 'What can you do?' asked the Personnel Manager.
'Lots,' replied the young man. 'I can play golf, talk

with a public school accent, make boring speeches, have affairs with secretaries without my wife finding out, go to sleep in the back of a Rolls Royce, and generally get publicity for working as hard as possible while in reality doing nothing at all.'

'Excellent!' said the Personnel Manager. 'You can start tomorrow as Managing Director.'

122. Jim's wife was chatting to her friend about Jim's boss, who at that moment was regaling the party with details of his war experiences in Egypt.

'I believe he's great at doing impressions,' commented the friend.

'Yes,' agreed Jim's wife. 'Right now he's doing his impression of a river – small at the head and big at the mouth.'

123. Office manager: 'Sir?'

Boss: 'Yes? What is it now?'

Office manager: 'Please sir, can I have a day off next week to do some late Christmas shopping with my wife and our six kids?'

Boss: 'Certainly not!'

Office manager: 'I knew you'd be understanding, sir. Thanks for getting me out of that terrible chore!'

124. Office junior: 'Please, sir, can I have a day off next month?'

Boss: 'What for?'

Office junior: 'I'm getting married.'

Boss: 'But you only earn thirty pounds a week; you look like a tramp; and you've no hope of ever rising above being an office junior. What sort of idiot would marry you?'

Office junior: 'Your daughter, sir.'

125. A man was visiting a workmate in hospital. 'You've been missed at the factory, Bill. Everybody's been talking about you. Why, only the other day the boss said to me: "What's happened to what's his name?"'

BUILDERS/WORKERS

126. The town council had requested tenders to build a monument in the town square. Only three tenders arrived on the town clerk's desk and he interviewed them all.

The first builder gave a tender of £3,000, broken down thus: £1,000 for him, £1,000 for materials and £1,000 for workmen.

The second builder gave a tender of £6,000: £2,000 for him, £2,000 for materials and £2,000 for the workmen.

The third builder gave his tender of £9,000 and when asked how he would break it down replied: 'I'd give £3,000 to you, £3,000 for me . . . and I'll give the job to the first tender!'

127. A man was laying a new concrete path. No sooner was his back turned than a crowd of children came running, leaving footmarks all over the hardening surface. A neighbour, who heard him swearing, reproached him: 'I thought you liked children, George.'

'I do like them,' he replied, 'in the abstract, but not in the concrete.'

128. Builder: 'I thought I recognized your daughter, sir. She was in the school that I was doing some work on. In the first year, I believe.'

Harassed man: 'And which year was she in when you had finished the work?'

129. We hear a lot about bad workmanship in building these days but the following story wants some swallowing. A workman called out from a room in one of the houses being built to a fellow workman in an adjoining house: 'Testing, Bill. Can you hear me?'

'Hear you?' replied the other, 'I can see you in three places!'

130. Three friendly scaffolders were having a chat over their morning break. Fred opened his lunchbox, opened up a sandwich and gave a scowl. 'Ham again!' he protested. 'It was ham on Monday, ham on Tuesday and now ham again. If it's ham again tomorrow I'm going to throw myself off this scaffold.'

Joe opened his lunchbox. 'Cheese again!' he protested. 'It's been cheese all week.' He threatened to do the same as Fred.

Patrick opened his lunchbox and gazed forlornly at his jam sandwiches and made a pact with his two friends that if it was repeated tomorrow he would jump off the scaffold with them.

Tomorrow came and the lunchboxes were examined closely and, lo and behold, the same fillers lay between the sandwiches. Holding hands, they decided they would jump together.

At the inquest the tale of just why they had jumped came out and Fred's tearful wife blamed herself for not being more thoughtful. Joe's wife told the coroner that her husband had only complained about the cheese once and she thought that he was joking.

Mrs Finnigan jumped up and faced the coroner. 'I don't understand this at all,' she said. 'My Patrick always made his own sandwiches!'

131. Three lunatics were working on a building site, supposedly digging a trench. After a few hours the foreman came along and was surprised to find one of the men digging furiously while the other two were standing motionless, their shovels in the air, and claiming that they were both lamp posts. The foreman sacked the two men immediately and told them to go home. But the man in the trench also stopped work.

'It's all right,' said the foreman. 'I haven't fired you. You were working very well, so carry on.'

'How?' asked the man. 'How do you expect me to work in the dark?'

132. Some workers were busy on a construction site next to a toy shop when suddenly they hit granite while digging a trench. They urgently needed some picks, but their base was about 45 miles away and all the workmen were being paid a bonus for speedy completion of the work. What could they do?

Fortunately the toy shop had a large display in one of their windows in which life-size teddy bears appeared to be working in a coal mine. Each teddy bear clutched a pick in its paws.

The construction workers approached the toy shop owner and he agreed to let them borrow the picks for the rest of the day; the workmen promising to use their own picks the following day.

After working for about 3 hours very successfully, the workmen stopped for a brief lunch.

Unfortunately, when they returned, they found that all the picks had been stolen – to which a passer-by commented: 'Didn't you know that today's the day the teddy bears have their picks nicked?'

133. An experienced building labourer was placed in charge of the giant cement mixer when from the corner of his eye he spotted a human body hurtling through the sky and into the cement mixer. Immediately he switched off the machine but alas too late for the poor guy caught inside it.

He shouted for his friend to hurry across so that he could share the news. 'It's our friend Indian Joe,' he stammered. 'He must have slipped from the scaffold.'

Of course, the authorities had to be informed and in less than ten minutes a police car entered the builders' yard. The police officer came across and proceeded to take notes. 'We are sure that it's our Indian friend,' the officer was told. 'We were great mates and used to go for a drink together every lunch time at the pub down the road.'

The officer wanted the whole contents of the cement mixer tipped out and after examining the contents now spewed onto the ground proceeded to move his boot amidst the broken bones, flesh and part limbs.

'Did he have any distinguishing marks?' asked the officer.

'He had two rectums,' one of the men said, looking at the other for confirmation.

'How do you mean, he had two rectums?' the officer asked.

'Well, we told you that we used to have a drink with him at the pub down the road.' The officer nodded. 'The last time we were in there with him I heard the landlady say to her husband: "The Indian gentleman's just come in with the two arseholes".'

134. A man arrived at the Pearly Gates and on being asked his name, replied: 'Charlie Grabhall.'

'I don't think we have any notice of your coming,' he was informed. 'What was your occupation in earthly life?'

'Scrap metal merchant,' the visitor said.

'Oh,' said the angel. 'I will go and inquire.'

When he returned Charlie Grabhall had disappeared. So had the Pearly Gates!

135. It was the coldest day in Britain yesterday for the past twenty years. At Brighton, three mechanics were sitting in a garage, shivering, when they heard a knock at the door. On opening the door, the wind howled past them and they saw a shaking, shivering monkey who looked up and said: 'Excuse me, do you do welding?'

136. Two strangers wandered into a Working Men's Club in Wales and after ordering a drink sat a little distance from the pool table. Being a little curious as to how the other half lived, their eyes scanned the whole room which was well attended. One man's eye caught sight of Evan Jones standing at the bar. The peculiar thing about Evan was that his head was absolutely flat, which caused the stranger to laugh. The first stranger pointed out the peculiar sight of a man with a flat head to his friend and he, too, joined in the laughter.

This rudeness was not unnoticed by Evan's friends who quickly came to his defence.

'I hope that you aren't laughing at Evan,' said club member David, towering over the table. The two went silent. 'Because Evan is the bravest man in here. Do you know,' David went on, 'that man saved the lives of hundreds of miners.'

'How?' asked the now deflated visitors.

'Evan held the whole roof up with his head,' they were told.

'And how did he get that cauliflower ear?' they wanted to know.

'That's where we hit him with the hammer when we were wedging him in,' he told the amazed pair.

CIVIL SERVICE

137. How many Civil Servants does it take to change a light bulb?

Twenty-two: ten to form a committee, five to form a sub committee, three to form a working party, two to hold the ladder, one to put in the bulb and one to write the report.

138. Have you heard about the man who had an addiction to red tape?

He joined the Civil Service.

139. How do you pay a Civil Servant ten times what he's worth?

Privatise his department and give him share options.

140. John rushed out of the committee room and almost collided with Colin.

'Quick,' he said, 'where's the tea lady? An important meeting is going on and we need . . .'

'Refreshment?' finished Colin for him.

'No, the tea leaves! They need to make a decision and we've lost the pin and blindfold they usually use!'

141. Why do Civil Servants never talk about their work?

Because they never do any.

142. 'I hear that your son unearthed a skull whilst playing last week.'

'Yes. It was the thickest skull that I've ever seen, so we've sent it to the council!'

143. I went to the Council. I said: 'I've come about my roof.'

He said: 'What about your roof?'

I said: 'I want one!'

144. When James graduated from Oxford he applied for a position in the Civil Service. At his selection interview he was asked: 'What can you do well?'

James thought for a moment and then replied: 'Nothing.'

'Good!' cried the selection panel in unison. 'You're just the sort of chap we want – and we won't even have to break you in!'

145. The senior civil servant went to the doctor and complained of being unable to sleep.

Doctor: 'Oh! Don't you sleep at night?'

Civil Servant: 'Yes, I sleep very well at night. And I sleep quite soundly most of the mornings, too – but I find it's very difficult to sleep in the afternoons as well.'

146. A surgeon, a Field Marshal and a politician had had a very liquid lunch together and were now in a deep argument.

'A surgeon's job is the oldest profession in the world,' said the surgeon.

'What makes you say that?' asked the Field Marshal.

'Well,' replied the surgeon. 'When woman was created she was made from one of Adam's ribs and surely only a surgeon could do something like that.'

'Nonsense!' snorted the Field Marshal. 'Even before Adam and Eve there was a world and it is said that order was created out of chaos. Who else could do that but a soldier of the highest rank?'

'Ah!' said the politician. 'But who do you think created the chaos to be sorted out?'

147. The aspiring spy was being interviewed in Whitehall by a Secret Service Chief, who was explaining the sort of men he looked for.

'We need people who are more than just involved,' he said. 'In this game you have to be committed. It is rather like the difference between bacon and eggs. So far as the chicken is concerned with the production of this marvellous start to the day – well, she *is* involved; but the pig, *he* is committed!'

148. 'Now,' said the interviewer, 'before we start the interview proper I'd like you to take an intelligence test.'

'An intelligence test?' queried the job applicant. 'The advertisement in the newspaper didn't mention intelligence – it stated you were looking for a research assistant for an MP.'

CLOTHES & FASHION

149. A Scotsman was fined for indecent conduct at Edinburgh on Friday. According to witnesses the man had continually wiped the perspiration off his forehead with his kilt.

150. Two women met and one said: 'I didn't know that your boy had to wear glasses.'

'Well, he doesn't have to really,' replied the other, 'but they were his poor dear father's and it seems a pity to waste them.'

151. 'Do you like my new hairstyle?' cooed the trendy young girl to her somewhat conservative boyfriend.

'Well,' he said, 'it reminds me of a beautiful Italian dish.'

'An actress?' she inquired eagerly.

'No. Spaghetti.'

152. A man walked through the streets of Southampton today wearing only a newspaper. He said he liked to dress with *The Times*.

153. The latest fashion news from Paris is that skirts will remain the same length as last year – but legs will be shorter.

154. Tommy found the old, abandoned family Bible in the attic and opened it to find a large leaf pressed between its heavy pages. 'Oh,' he said. 'Adam must have left his clothes here.'

155. Mavis: 'On the way to work this morning a man stopped me in the street and showed me the lining of his raincoat.'

Claudia: 'Are you sure he only wanted you to see his raincoat?'

Mavis: 'Oh, yes! He wasn't wearing anything else.'

156. It was a lovely warm evening and a business man who had just come from the City thought that he would take a quiet dip in the sea. There appeared to be no one about so he undressed quickly and slipped into the water. After a very enjoyable bathe he came out and to his horror found that, with the exception of his bowler hat, his clothes had been stolen. Well, there was no help for it, so holding his bowler in front, he walked quickly up the beach hoping to find someone he knew and could help him.

Suddenly there appeared two ladies whom he knew slightly and to whom he merely bowed. One of the ladies who was elderly and short-sighted asked: 'Who was that who passed us so hurriedly?'

'Oh, that was Mr Jones,' came the reply from the other lady.

'Well,' said the first, 'he was no gentleman or he would have raised his hat.'

'Well, I think that he was because he didn't,' came the reply.

157. A young man purchased a large grandfather clock from an antique shop in Brighton.

He put the unwrapped clock over his shoulder and began to look for a taxi. He hailed one approaching from the right but it ignored him, so, swinging around, he tried to flag one down approaching from the left. Unfortunately, as he turned around the clock over his shoulder struck an old lady on the head and she fell into the gutter.

'Idiot!' she shrieked. 'Why can't you wear a normal wrist-watch like the rest of us?'

DEFINITIONS

158. Adolescence – period in life between puberty and adultery.

159. Adults – people who have stopped growing at the ends but have started to grow in the middle.

160. Bacteria – the back entrance of a cafeteria.

161. Blunderbuss – a coach load of spinsters on their way to a maternity hospital.

162. Buoyant – male equivalent of gallant.

163. Catacomb – a comb for a cat.

164. Cloak – mating call of a Chinese frog.

165. Countdown – something they do in an eiderdown factory.

166. Dogma – the mother of puppies.

167. Eunuch – man cut out to be a bachelor.

168. Gentleman – one who gives up his seat to a lady in a public convenience.

169. Ghoulash – a cremated ghost.

170. Mistress – something between a mister and a mattress.

171. Mushroom – place where Eskimos train their dogs.

172. Myth – unmarried female with a lisp.

173. Octopus – an eight-sided cat.

174. Polysyllables – the language of parrots.

175. Sadist – someone who would put a drawing-pin on an electric chair.

176. Signature tune – song of a young swan.

177. Statistician – a person who, if you've got your feet in the oven and your head in the refrigerator, will tell you that, on average, you're very comfortable.

178. Ultimate – the last person to marry.

179. Vice versa – dirty poems.

DOCTORS/HEALTH

180. 'Doctor, I wish to protest about the spare-part surgery operation you did on me.'

'What's wrong? I gave you another hand when your own was smashed up at your factory.'

'I know. But you gave me a female hand which is very good most of the time – it's only that whenever I go to the toilet it doesn't want to let go.'

181. Patient: 'Doctor, I think I've got an inferiority complex.'

Doctor: 'Don't be silly. You really are inferior.'

182. Doctor: 'How do you feel today?'

Patient: 'With my hands – just like I usually do.'

183. Doctor examining a patient: 'What's that strange growth on your neck?' (Pause) 'Oh – it's your head.'

184. The only reason doctors wear masks when they perform operations is so that no one can recognise them if anything goes wrong.

185. Pretty nurse to Doctor: 'Every time I take this patient's pulse, it seems to beat faster. What shall I do?'

Doctor: 'Blindfold him!'

186. Doctor: 'Miss Smith, you have acute appendicitis.'

Miss Smith: 'I came here to be examined – not admired.'

187. Patient: 'Doctor, doctor! What do I need for in-growing toenails?'
Doctor: 'In-growing toes.'

188. Doctor: 'Have you ever had your eyes checked?'
Patient: 'No, doctor. They've always been brown.'

189. 'Nurse, is it true that uncooked eels are healthy?'
'I imagine so, sir. I've never heard any complaining.'

190. There was a very high pitched scream from the operating theatre, and then the doctor's voice could be heard: 'Nurse! I said take off the patient's *spec*tacles.'

191. 'Doctor! I think I've just taken a turn for the nurse!'

192. 'Well, how do you find yourself these cold, winter mornings?'
'Oh, I just throw back the blankets and there I am.'

193. Doctor: 'And how are we this morning?'
Patient: 'I'm feeling better doctor, but my breathing still troubles me.'
Doctor: 'We must see if we can put a stop to that.'

194. Late one night a doctor received a telephone call from a man who said urgently: 'Doctor, my mother-in-law is lying at death's door. Can you come round and pull her through?'

195. Molly, one of the nurses in the hospital, was always going around joking and laughing and teasing the patients.
Knowing Molly's sense of fun, one of the male patients named John decided to play a little trick on her.
When asked to provide a specimen of his urine he

took some orange squash which his mother had brought for him and poured this into the bottle instead.

When Molly came to collect the sample, John made as if to hand the bottle over to her – but then said: 'Hmm. It looks a bit weak. I'd better pass it through again.'

He then put the bottle to his lips and drank the contents. Molly fainted.

196. 1st patient: 'I see they've brought in another case of diarrhoea.'

2nd patient: 'That's good! Anything is better than that awful lemonade they've been giving us.'

197. A man entered hospital for an appendicitis operation. When he came round afterwards he mentioned to the nurse that his throat felt terribly sore.

'Oh,' she said, 'perhaps I had better explain. You see, at your operation this morning there were a number of medical students present and when the surgeon had finished they were so impressed that they applauded him; so for an encore he took out your tonsils.'

198. The medical student was accompanying one of the consultants on his hospital rounds. Time after time, the student made a completely wrong diagnosis.

'Have you ever thought about taking up a different career?' asked the consultant. 'One where you would not be fired for frequent mis-diagnoses – such as a government economist?'

199. 1st student: 'Why are you saving all those old magazines?'

2nd student: 'Because I qualify as a doctor in five years' time and I'll need something suitable for my waiting room.'

200. Patient: 'And if I take these little green pills exactly as you suggested, will I get better?'

Doctor: 'Well, let's put it this way – none of my patients has ever come back for more of those pills.'

201. Nurse: 'Can I take your pulse?'

Patient: 'Why? Haven't you got one of your own?'

202. 'Doctor, doctor! I'm terribly worried. I keep seeing pink striped crocodiles every time I try to get to sleep.'

'Have you seen a psychiatrist?'

'No – only pink striped crocodiles.'

203. The same question was put to three different men: 'If you were told by your doctor that you had only one month longer to live, what would you do?'

The first man replied: 'I would set about putting my affairs in order, lead a quiet, peaceful life, and prepare for the end.'

The next man said: 'I would realize all my assets, have a right good time and then I wouldn't mind what happened.'

The third man merely said: 'I should consult another doctor.'

204. She's so stupid she spent hours in the library trying to study for her blood test.

205. When Chris swallowed a boomerang he returned home from hospital and was re-admitted ninety-eight times.

206. Sarah: 'Why are you walking like a crab?'

Jane: 'It's these new pills I'm taking – they have side effects.'

207. Tom: 'Darling, I know you're pregnant and that

pregnant women often get strange cravings. But do you really have to eat so many old rubber tyres?'

Sandra: 'But I'm only trying to make sure we have a bouncing baby.'

208. 'Doctor, it's impossible for my wife to be pregnant. I'm a sailor and I've been away from her working on my ship overseas for more than a year.'

'I know. But it's what we call a "grudge pregnancy". Someone had it in for you.'

209. Doctor: 'Why do you think you've become schizophrenic?'

Patient: 'It was the only way I could think of to prove that two could live as cheaply as one.'

210. 'Yes,' one man said to another. 'I've read so much about smoking causing various illnesses that I've decided to give up reading!'

211. The doctor was visiting 78-year-old Jim at his home to give him a routine check-up.

'For a man of your age,' said the doctor, 'you're in excellent shape. How do you manage it?'

'Well,' replied Jim, 'I don't drink, I don't smoke and I've never played around with women and . . .' He was interrupted by a crashing sound and female shrieks coming from the room immediately above them.

'What was that?' asked the doctor.

'Oh!' said Jim, 'Only my father chasing the new au pair girl. He must be drunk again!'

212. The Red Indian who always suffered from colds was named Running Nose.

213. One of the elves was getting rather fat, so his wife sent him away to the Elf Farm.

214. Doctor: 'Did you do as I directed and take your medicine after your bath?'

Patient: 'I tried to, doctor, but after drinking the bath I didn't really have room to drink the medicine as well.'

215. Doctor: 'Nurse! Did you take this patient's temperature?'

Nurse: 'Why, doctor? Is it missing?'

216. Nurse: 'Doctor, why are you trying to write that prescription with a thermometer?'

Absent-minded doctor: 'Drat! Some silly bum must have my biro!'

217. The pompous patient had annoyed everyone in the ward. The nurses were tired of his amorous advances at them, and the other patients had rapidly become irritated with his highly detailed boasts of his probably fictional conquests of numerous women.

One young nurse decided to teach the man a lesson.

'Now, sir, I want to take your temperature as the doctor instructed,' she explained. 'So I'll just close the screens around your bed and then you must take your pyjamas off.'

'Oh, ho, ho!' said the man, loudly. 'So you fancy a bit of slap and tickle with Mr Fantastic himself, eh? Fancy asking me to take my pyjamas off just to take my temperature! A likely story!'

'I'm serious,' insisted the nurse. 'The doctor has ordered a rectal temperature to be taken.'

'You mean, you want to stick the thermometer up my . . .'

'Yes,' replied the nurse hastily.

Soon the screens were in position around the man's bed, his pyjamas were removed, and the nurse carried out her plan.

'There, I'll have to leave the thermometer in position

45

for a few minutes,' said the nurse, and left the enclosure around the bed.

For the next five minutes the ward was filled with muffled giggles and shrieks of laughter.

'What's all the noise?' asked the matron, entering the ward and noticing a lot of nurses and patients peering in through gaps in the screens around the man.

On entering the enclosure around the man's bed, the matron demanded of the man: 'What is the reason for this?'

'For what?' asked the man. 'The nurse is taking my temperature.'

'With *this*? demanded the matron, taking a tulip out of the man's behind to the accompaniment of riotous laughter from the onlookers who were still peering in through the screens.

218. On the promenade of the famous health resort at Vichy, two women visitors were listening to an orchestra playing Haydn's Farewell Symphony. In this piece one player after another lays down his instrument and tiptoes away. The women watched in astonishment as the last musician disappeared, leaving the conductor alone before the empty chairs.

Then one of the women whispered to the other: 'I don't wonder at it,' she said compassionately. 'It's the effect of all that Vichy water.'

219. Nurse: 'Well, Mr Mitchell, you seem to be coughing much more easily this morning.'

Mr Mitchell, groaning in his bed: 'That's because I've been practising all night.'

220. 'Doctor, I'm worried about my wife. She thinks she's a bird.'

'Well, you had better bring her in to see me.'

'I can't. She's just flown south for winter.'

221. Stockbroker patient: 'Tell me, nurse, what is my temperature?'

Nurse: 'A hundred and one.'

Stockbroker patient: 'When it gets to a hundred and two – sell.'

222. Patient: 'Doctor, my wooden leg keeps giving me the most awful pain.'

Doctor: 'Don't be ridiculous! How can a wooden leg give you pain?'

Patient: 'My wife keeps hitting me on the head with it.'

223. Patient: 'Doctor, why did the receptionist rush out of the room screaming?'

Doctor: 'When she asked you to strip to the waist ready for my examination she meant you to strip from the neck down, not from the toes up!'

224. 'I've got some good news and some bad news. I'll give you the bad news first but if you don't want to hear it, close your eyes!'

225. 'Martha!' shouted frail little Sidney from his bed. 'I'm terribly sick, please call me a vet.'

'A vet?' queried Martha. 'Why do you want a vet and not a doctor?'

'Because,' replied Sidney, 'I work like a horse, live like a dog, and have to sleep with a silly cow!'

226. A boy entered a chemist's shop and asked for a box of pills. 'Certainly,' said the chemist and then, wishing to be helpful, asked 'Antibilious?'

'No,' replied the boy. 'They're for Uncle.'

227. A man went for a brain transplant and was offered the choice of two brains – an architect's for £10,000 and a politician's for £100,000.

'Does that mean the politician's brain is much better than the architect's?' asked the man.

'Not exactly,' replied the brain transplant salesman. 'The politician's has never been used.'

228. A man who had a reputation as a road-hog was lying semi-conscious in a hospital bed.

'How is he this morning?' the doctor inquired.

'Oh,' replied the nurse, 'he keeps putting out his right arm.'

'Ah!' remarked the doctor genially. 'He's turning the corner.'

229. Doctor to patient: 'You are a great deal better this morning, I see. You evidently followed my instructions and the prescription must have worked wonders. But you haven't taken any of the medicine!'

Patient: 'No. You see, it says on the label – keep the bottle tightly corked.'

230. Voice on the phone: 'Hello? Is that the maternity hospital?'

Receptionist: 'Yes.'

Voice on the phone: 'Can you send an ambulance round, the wife is about to have a baby.'

Receptionist: 'Is this her first baby?'

Voice on the phone: 'No. This is her husband.'

231. A doctor and his wife were sitting in deck chairs on the beach when a beautiful young girl in a very brief bikini jogged towards them. As she came to the doctor she waved at him and said, in a huskily sexy voice: 'Hi, there!' before continuing on her way.

'Who was that?' demanded the doctor's wife.

'Oh, just someone I met professionally,' replied the doctor.

'Oh, yes!' snorted the wife. 'Whose profession? Yours or hers?'

232. The man staggered into the doctor's surgery. He had three knives protruding out of his back, his head was bleeding from a gunshot wound, and his legs had been badly beaten by a hockey stick.

The doctor's receptionist looked up at this pitiful sight and said: 'Do you have an appointment?'

233. The patient who had just come round after an operation was recovering in a ward and heard two other patients talking. Said one: 'Some of these surgeons are a bit forgetful. They left a swab in one chap and he had to be opened up again to remove it.'

'Yes,' replied the other, 'I heard that, and there was another patient who had a scalpel left in him.'

At that moment the surgeon who had performed the operation on the new patient popped his head round the door and asked: 'Has anyone seen my hat?' and the poor chap fainted.

234. The doctor had just finished examining the very attractive young girl.

Doctor: 'Have you been going out with men, Miss Jones?'

Miss Jones: 'Oh no, doctor, never!'

Doctor: 'Are you sure? Bearing in mind that I've now examined the sample you sent, do you still say you've never had anything to do with men?'

Miss Jones: 'Quite sure doctor. Can I go now?'

Doctor: 'No.'

Miss Jones: 'Why not?'

Doctor: 'Because, Miss Jones, I'm awaiting the arrival of the Three Wise Men.'

235. It was three o'clock in the morning and the plumber's telephone rang. It was the doctor, saying that his toilet seemed to have broken and could the plumber come immediately and fix it.

The plumber reluctantly agreed to visit the doctor's

house, although the plumber warned his client that at this time of the night he could only expect him to provide 'a doctor's treatment'.

When he arrived, the plumber went straight to the offending toilet, threw an asprin down it, and then said to the doctor: 'If it's not better by lunchtime tomorrow, phone me and I'll come again.'

236. Patient: 'Doctor, you've already said that the operation is very risky. What are my chances of survival?'

Doctor: 'Excellent! The odds against success are 99 to 1, but the surgeon who will be performing the operation on you is looking forward to it as you will be his hundredth patient and so you must be a success after all the others.'

237. Doctor: 'I can't find anything wrong with you, it must be the drink.'

Patient: 'Oh, I'll come back when you are sober.'

238. A man walked into the chemists. 'Have you got something to keep my stomach in?' he asked.

The assistant went round the back and brought out a wheelbarrow.

239. Patient: 'I've got bananas growing out of my ears.'

Doctor: 'Good gracious! How did that happen?'

Patient: 'I beg your pardon?'

240. Patient: 'Doctor! My head feels all stuffed up, my sinuses are blocked, and my waterworks don't work properly.'

Doctor: 'It seems to me that you'd be better off visiting a plumber instead of me.'

241. Patient: 'Doctor! I keep thinking I'm a chicken.'

Doctor: 'How long have you thought that?'

Patient: 'For about a year.'

Doctor: 'Why didn't you come and see me earlier?'

Patient: 'Because my wife said we needed the eggs.'

242. 'When I stand up quickly I see Donald Duck and Pluto and when I bend suddenly I see Mickey Mouse and Popeye.'

'Oh,' said the doctor, 'and how long have you been having these Disney spells?'

243. Patient: 'Doctor, doctor! I keep talking to myself.'

Doctor: 'That's nothing to worry about. Lots of people mutter to themselves.'

Patient: 'But I'm a life assurance salesman and I keep selling myself policies I don't want.'

244. American doctor: 'I don't know how to put this, but if I recommended that you had an operation, would you be able to pay for it?'

American patient: 'If I couldn't pay for it, would you still recommend that I had the operation, or some other cure?'

245. A man was waiting at a hospital to see a doctor. When he saw a white-coated figure approaching he asked anxiously: 'Are you a doctor?'

'No,' came the reply. 'Actually I'm a student passing out as a doctor.'

This happened again a few minutes later with the same reply to his question. When a third white-coated figure appeared the visitor was becoming despondent and said: 'I suppose you're a student also, passing out as a doctor.'

'Oh, no,' the newcomer said. 'I'm a painter, passing out for a pint!'

246. Mother: 'My son can't stop biting nails.'

Doctor: 'How old is your son?'

Mother: 'Fifteen.'

Doctor: 'That's not unusual. Even at his age some people still bite their nails when they're nervous . . .'

Mother (interrupting): 'But he bites long nails he's pulled out of the floorboards!'

247. A Scotsman was seriously ill in hospital and his last request was for the bagpipes to be played. They were. He recovered; the other patients died.

248. Visitor: 'Excuse me, but can you tell me which ward Vera Ogglebuggy is in?'

Receptionist: 'Ah, yes. Wasn't she the lady who was run down by a steamroller earlier this morning?'

Visitor: 'Yes.'

Receptionist: 'Well, she's in Wards 7, 8, 9, 10 and 11.'

249. Doctor: 'I'm afraid your records haven't reached me yet from your previous doctor and my scales have just been broken by an enormously fat lady patient of mine. But can you tell me your average weight?'

Patient: 'I'm sorry, I don't know.'

Doctor: 'Do you know the most you have weighed?'

Patient: 'I think it was twelve stone nine pounds.'

Doctor: 'And what was the least you've weighed?'

Patient: 'I think that was about seven pounds three ounces.'

250. The telephone rings and matron answers it: 'Yes, hello. You want to know how Mr Gough is doing? His operation seemed to go extremely well and we have every hope that he can leave the hospital soon. Might I know who is speaking so I can pass on your interest and concern to him?'

The voice on the phone answers: 'This *is* Mr Gough.

They don't tell patients themselves *anything* in this place!'

251. When a patient came to after an operation he noticed that a screen had been placed round his bed.

'What's the idea of the screen?' he asked. 'Didn't you expect me to recover?'

'Oh, it's not that,' said the doctor. 'You see, during the operation the premises opposite caught fire and burst into flames and we didn't want you to think that the worst had happened.'

252. A labourer was working near a guillotine when he bent over a little too far and his ear was severed. Man and ear were quickly rushed to the hospital.

Whilst his injury was being cleaned up in one ward, the ear was being prepared for micro surgery until both he and his ear came once again together. The ear lay on a tray and the sight of it made the labourer suspicious. 'That's not *my* ear,' he protested. 'My ear had a cigarette behind it!'

253. A man walked into the offices of a plastic surgeon and handed over a cheque for two thousand pounds to the receptionist.

'I think there is some mistake,' said the receptionist. 'Your bill is only one thousand pounds.'

'I know,' replied the man, 'but the operation was tremendously successful. The surgeon took some skin from my behind – where no one will ever see that it's missing – and grafted it on to my cheek and totally got rid of the large scar I used to have there.'

'So the extra thousand is for a job well done,' said the receptionist.

'Not exactly. It's a token of appreciation for all the delight I get every time my mother-in-law kisses my backside – and doesn't even know it!'

254. An excited father at a hospital said to the nurse: 'Quick, tell me, is it a boy?'

The nurse tried to break it to him gently. 'Well,' she replied, 'the one in the middle is!'

255. He was so ugly that when he was born the midwife slapped his father!

256. Patient: 'Doctor! Can you give me anything to stop me from sleepwalking?'

Doctor: 'Here's a box of a special item that should solve your problem. After you've got into bed for the night, sprinkle the contents of the box on the floor around your bed.'

Patient: 'What's in the box, doctor? Is it a powder that gives off a special odour?'

Doctor: 'No. Inside the box are drawing pins.'

257. The Prince of Wales was visiting a hospital and was directed into the men's ward. Shaking hands with the patient in the first bed he asked him what he was in for. 'Piles,' he was told. The Prince asked what the treatment was. 'Wire brush and liquid paraffin,' was the reply. 'And what is your chief ambition?' the patient was asked. 'To be an airline pilot,' he replied.

The Prince moved on to the next patient and was surprised to hear that he too was suffering from piles and was undergoing the same treatment.

He moved to the next bed. 'Are you also suffering from piles?' the third patient was asked.

'Laryngitis,' croaked the patient.

'What is the treatment for that?' the Prince wanted to know.

'The same,' said the patient. 'Wire brush and liquid paraffin.'

'And what is your chief ambition?' asked a sympathetic Prince.

'To get that wire brush before the other two,' he was told.

258. George was called to the doctors for a check-up, but the real reason for his recall was to give him some advice.

'How many children have you now, George?' the doctor asked.

'I've got eleven, doctor, at the last count. Not a bad score for a life's work!' George boasted.

'It's about time you thought about your partner,' the doctor scolded. 'Any more children could kill her,' he warned.

George's smile moved from his face as he heeded the warning. 'We won't have any more. If she has any more I'll hang myself.'

Time moved on and George's wife confessed that she was pregnant again. When she was out doing the shopping, George fitted a hook into the ceiling and slung a rope over it. Standing on the chair with the rope around his neck, a thought entered his head which made him remove the rope. 'Hold on a bit,' he told himself. 'I might be hanging the wrong man!'

259. The medical lecturer in the newly opened Medical School turned to one of his pupils and said: 'Now, Jones, it is clear from this X-ray I am holding up that one of this patient's legs is considerably shorter than the other. This, of course, accounts for the patient's limp. But what would *you* do in a case like this?'

Jones thought for a few seconds, then said brightly: 'I should imagine, sir, that I would limp, too.'

260. Handsome young man, from behind a screen: 'I've taken all my clothes off, nurse. Where shall I put them?'

Young nurse: 'On top of mine.'

261. Did you hear about the doctor who tried to be a kidnapper? He failed because no one could read his ransom letters.

262. A fashionable society doctor received an urgent call and when he arrived and asked what was the matter, the lady of the house said: 'It's the maid. She is in bed and refuses to get up.'

'Perhaps I had better have a few words with her alone,' said the doctor. So he went up the stairs and, entering the room, found the maid in bed as her mistress had said.

'Now,' said the doctor, 'what's the trouble?'

'There's no trouble,' said the maid, 'but I haven't been paid my wages for six weeks, so I am not getting up until they have been paid.'

'Right,' said the doctor, and he started to take off his clothes.

'Here!' cried the maid. 'What are you up to?'

'Nothing,' he replied, 'but just move over. They owe me for a twelvemonth.'

263. Old Bill Jenkins had made an appointment to see the doctor because, of late, his innards had been giving him some concern. But due to his deafness he had to ask his wife, Emily, along so that she could interpret all that the doctor said. His name was called in the surgery and in before the doctor they both went.

'What's the matter?' asked the doctor.

'It's his innards again,' answered Emily. Bill looked at his wife. 'I'm telling him it's your innards' she informed him. Bill nodded.

'I had best give him a full examination.' A full examination was conveyed to Bill.

The doctor undid the two top buttons of Bill's shirt and inserted his stethoscope. Emily shouted down Bill's ear to breathe in and out.

'Does he smoke?' asked the doctor.

'He wants to know if you smoke,' Emily shouted. Bill shook his head.

'I thought not,' said the doctor, 'his lungs are quite clear. Does he take a drink?'

'Do you drink?' the question was conveyed to Bill whose eyes lit up.

'There's nothing wrong with his throat then,' the doctor seemed relieved. 'What I would like is a sample of his motion and his urine,' instructed the doctor. 'You can leave them at reception when you've got them.'

Bill fidgeted on his chair. 'What did he say?' he wanted to know.

'We have to leave your underpants at reception,' she told him.

264. Simon was worried about his ever increasing weight. One day in his club he happened to mention this to his friend, Peter.

'I can recommend a very good doctor,' said Peter. 'I owe my slimness all to Dr Frank Einstein. He's invented these marvellous pills which I take.'

'It sounds quite amazing,' said Simon. 'But how do they work?'

'It's really psychological. Every night I take two of the pills just before going to sleep and I always dream about being on a South Sea island, surrounded by hordes of beautiful young native girls. And every day I chase them all around the island and when I wake up I seem to have sweated off a few ounces of surplus fat. It's incredible – and enjoyable!'

The following day Simon went to see Dr Einstein and begged him to give him the same tablets as he was giving Peter. The doctor agreed, and within a few weeks Simon was much thinner.

'How are you finding the treatment?' asked Dr Einstein, when Simon called in for his regular check-up.

'It's very good. But I do have one complaint.'

57

'Oh, and what is that?'

'The pills you gave my friend Peter made him have wonderful dreams about chasing young native girls all over an island. But all I seem to get is the same horrible nightmare – being chased all over the island by hungry cannibals. Why can't I have pleasant dreams like Peter?'

'Because,' replied the doctor, 'Peter is a private patient – and you are National Health.'

265. An elderly doctor took a young partner into his practice and said: 'I would like you to accompany me on my visits tomorrow so that you can observe my procedure, which you may care to adopt.' So the next day they set off. The first visit was to a rather plump lady, who was reclining in bed. After introducing his new partner, the old doctor took the patient's temperature but dropped the thermometer which he retrieved from under the bed where it had fallen.

As they prepared to depart he said: 'You know, Mrs Goodbody, you would recover much quicker if you didn't eat so many chocolates.' The patient blushed and they left.

When they were outside the house, the young doctor asked: 'How did you know about her eating chocolates?'

'Well,' replied the other, 'you saw me stoop down to pick up the thermometer? Under the bed were all the chocolate wrappings.'

At the next house a very elegant lady was sitting up in bed in readiness for their visit. So the old doctor said: 'I've brought along my new partner who will attend to you this morning Mrs Loveday.' Whereupon the young doctor proceeded to take the patient's temperature and he also dropped the thermometer which fell to the floor.

As they were leaving he said: 'You know, Mrs Loveday, you ought not to be taking quite so much interest in church affairs.'

When they had left the house, the old doctor asked: 'Why on earth did you say that about the church?'

'Well,' replied the doctor, 'I did the same as you; I dropped the thermometer and when I reached under the bed to pick it up, there was the vicar!'

266. An old farmer was passing through the town one day when he decided to pay a visit to the doctor.

'I should be most grateful,' said the farmer, 'if you would call in one day and take a look at my wife.'

'Certainly,' replied the doctor. 'Is your dear wife ill?'

'I don't really know,' said the farmer. 'But yesterday morning she got out of bed at the usual time of four o'clock in the morning and milked the cows and made breakfast for me and the farmhands; then did the farm accounts; made the dinner; churned the milk; fed the chickens; ploughed a few fields; then made the supper before repainting the living room – but about midnight she was complaining she was a bit tired. I think, doctor, she needs a bit of a tonic or something.'

267. A doctor was fuming when he finally reached his seat at a civic dinner, after breaking away from a woman who sought his advice on a personal health problem.

'Do you think I should send her a bill?' he asked a solicitor who sat next to him.

'Why not?' the solicitor replied. 'You rendered professional service by giving her advice.'

'Thanks,' the physician said, 'I think I'll do that.'

When the doctor went to his surgery next day to send the bill to the woman, he found a letter from the solicitor. It read: 'For legal services, £50'.

268. The eminent surgeon was walking through his local churchyard one day when he saw the gravedigger having a rest and drinking from a bottle of beer.

'Hey, you!' called the surgeon. 'How dare you laze about and drink alcohol in the churchyard! Get on with your job, or I shall complain to the vicar.'

'I should have thought you'd be the last person to complain,' said the gravedigger, 'bearing in mind all your blunders I've had to cover up.'

269. Penicillin – the present for the man who has everything.

270. 'Roll up! Roll up! Buy this miraculous cure for old age and colds. Rigor mortis can be cured! Roll up! Roll up!' called the fairground quack doctor.

He soon collected a large crowd around his stall, and the quack went on to proclaim the merits of his products. 'This miraculous mixture actually cures old age. You have only to look at me to see the proof of its power. I am over two hundred and fifty years old.'

One astonished man in the crowd turned to the quack's beautiful young assistant and said: 'Say, miss, is what the gentleman says really true? Is he really over two hundred and fifty years old?'

'I'm afraid I can't really say,' replied the quack's assistant. 'I've only been working for him for the past ninety-three years.'

271. A man bought a hat and afterwards complained that when he put it on he could hear music. He mentioned it to his doctor who, deciding to humour him, gave him the address of a psychiatrist. The man called and explained his trouble, saying that whenever he wore the hat he could hear a tune being played. The psychiatrist took the hat and went into another room and, returning in a few moments said: 'Now try it on.'

The man did so and exclaimed: 'Wonderful! Music's gone! What did you do?'

Said the psychiatrist: 'I merely removed the band!'

272. Amelia didn't know what to do with her seven-year-old son, Mark. Every time a visitor came to the house or he saw someone he didn't know, he would race towards them and bite them on the knee. Then he would cling to their legs and refuse to let go.

In desperation, Amelia took her son to a child psychologist and on seeing the psychologist Mark rushed towards him, bit his knee and then clung on to the man's legs.

The child psychologist looked down at Mark, then bent and whispered something in the boy's ear. Immediately, Mark let go of the man's legs and ran back to his mother.

'He's cured!' cried Amelia. 'What did you say to him?'

The child psychologist smiled and said: 'I told him that if he didn't let go of my legs I'd smash his stupid face in.'

273. Then there was the psychiatrist who woke up one morning to find himself under his bed. He decided he was a little potty.

274. Question: What are the differences between psychologists, psychoanalysts and psychiatrists?

Answer: Psychologists build castles in the air, psychoanalysts live in them and psychiatrists collect the rent!

275. Patient: 'Doctor, doctor! I think I'm becoming invisible.'

Doctor: 'Who said that?'

276. He went into the opticians and said, 'I think my eyes are going.'

The reply he got was: 'They've gone, mate. This is a chip shop!'

277. I went into the chemist and said: 'Could I have 3 condoms, miss?'

She said: 'Don't *miss* me!'

I said: 'All right, make it 4.'

278. A man went into an American drugstore and bought a packet of contraceptives.

'That will be one dollar twenty cents – plus tax,' said the cashier.

'Don't bother with the tax,' said the man. 'I'll tie them on.'

279. 'I went to the dentist this morning.'

'Does your tooth still hurt?'

'I don't know – the dentist kept it.'

280. A rather nervous woman entered the dentist's surgery. 'I'd rather have a baby than have a tooth out' she said.

'Make your mind up quick,' said the dentist, 'because I'll have to adjust the chair.'

281. The woman patient confronted her doctor.

'There's nothing wrong with me,' she told him, 'but I'm worried about my husband.'

'Oh?' said the doctor, half expecting what was to come next.

'He's lost his sex drive,' she whimpered, 'and I wondered if you could help me put it back.'

The doctor rose, walked to his drug cabinet and counted out six little white pills. 'Ask him to take one of these each night before going to bed,' he instructed, 'and as they are a new type of pill, let me know as soon as they begin to work.'

With a new hope the woman left the surgery only to return the next day, with a broad smile across her face.

'They work, they work!' she confessed with glee. 'When he wasn't looking during yesterday's meal I popped all the six pills into his coffee cup. He made love to me at once upon the very chair he was sat on until the chair legs broke.'

'Oh?' said the alarmed doctor.

'Yes,' sighed the delighted woman. 'Then he threw me across the table and did it again until the table collapsed. And do you know something, doctor? There were scorch marks on the carpet where his knees had been.'

'I do apologise,' said the doctor.

'Apologise?' said the woman. 'They worked!'

'Yes,' he said. 'I was apologising for the damage.'

'That's all right, doctor,' she answered. 'We won't go to *that* restaurant again!'

DRINKS & PUBS

282. It was a dark, cloudy night and the drunk staggered into the cemetery and fell into a hole which had been dug in preparation for a burial the following day. The drunk hiccuped and fell asleep.

Half an hour later another drunk swayed into the cemetery. He was singing loudly and his raucous voice woke up the drunk in the grave who suddenly started to yell that he was cold.

The singing drunk tottered to the edge of the grave and peered blurrily down at the complaining drunk. 'It's no wonder you're cold,' he shouted down to the drunk. 'You've kicked all the soil off yourself.'

283. A very drunken man walked into a hotel and demanded a drink but the barman refused him, saying that he was too drunk to hold any more.

'I'm sober!' said the drunk. 'And I'll prove it! Do you see that cat coming through the door? Well it's only got one eye.'

'That proves you're drunk,' said that barman. 'That cat's not coming in . . . it's going out!'

284. Harry's wife heard the car draw up and looking through her bedroom window saw him carry three large bottles of beer into the house. She heard him come upstairs but when she looked out, couldn't see him on the landing. Pushing the bathroom door open she saw him pouring the three bottles of beer into the loo. When she asked about the incident he said it would save him getting up during the night.

285. A policeman on duty noticed a car being driven rather erratically down the road. It mounted the pavement on two occasions and then proceeded to turn into a road marked 'No Entry' and stopped dead. The policeman went over and said to the driver: 'And what do you think you're doing?'

The driver started to say something when his wife, who was sitting in the passenger seat beside him replied: 'Take no notice of him, officer, he's drunk!'

286. A drunk came across a man doing press ups in the park, so he said: 'Excuse me, I think someone has stolen your girlfriend.'

287. 'Help, help!' shouted the man in the sea. 'I can't swim!'

'So what?' shouted back a drunk man from the shore. 'I can't play the piano, but I'm not shouting about it.'

288. A man came up to me as I stood at the bar of this rough looking club. He said: 'I bet you're a stranger in here.'

I said: 'How do you know?'
He said: 'You've taken your hand off your glass!'

289. The landlord of a pub frequented by an extremely heavy drinker opened up one day, and in walked a pink elephant, a green rhinoceros and several orange striped crocodiles.

'I'm sorry,' said the publican, 'I'm afraid he isn't in yet.'

290. A gorilla walked into a quiet country pub and, putting down a £10 note, asked for a pint of bitter. The barman served him and thinking 'I bet he's a bit dim', gave him £5 in change. Then, wishing to appear friendly, said: 'We don't usually get many gorillas in here.'

'I bet you don't,' replied the gorilla, 'if you charge them £5 for a pint.'

291. A tramp walked into a public house and asked for a pint of beer. The landlord had just drawn it when the tramp said that he had changed his mind and could he have some bread and cheese instead. The publican kindly obliged him but when it came to payment, the tramp said that he really didn't owe anything as he had had the bread and cheese in exchange for the beer which he didn't drink.

The landlord realised that he had been 'had' but said to the tramp: 'Look, here is a pound. Go across the road to the other pub and play the same trick there.'

The tramp pocketed the money but when he got to the door he said: 'I think I should tell you that I've already been to the other pub and the landlord there gave me £5 to come across to you.'

292. The bride had got a little drunk and was having some difficulty in making her speech of thanks for all the wonderful wedding gifts.

At the end of her speech she pointed rather unsteadily towards an electric coffee percolator, and said: 'And, finally, I'd like to thank my husband's aunt for giving me such a lovely perky copulator.'

293. A police car flagged down a Volvo after trailing it for some time along a busy highway. Both cars pulled to the side of the road and a policeman walked slowly to the Volvo.

'I've been following you for some considerable time,' said the officer, 'and you've been swaying from one side of the road to the other.' He sniffed close to the driver. 'I've a bag here that says you've had too much to drink,' said the officer, moving his hand from behind his back.

The driver blinked in astonishment as his mouth fell agape. 'I've a bag at home to tell me that!' he told the officer.

294. The fire engine careered around the corner, and sped off up the road, bells clanging, just as a drunk was staggering out of a pub. He promptly chased after the fire engine, but soon collapsed, exhausted, after only a few hundred yards.

'All right,' he sobbed. 'You can keep your rotten ice lollies!'

295. The drunk staggered along the street with a large bottle of brandy in each pocket when he suddenly tripped and fell heavily on the ground.

As he began to pull himself to his feet he noticed that part of him felt wet. He touched the wet patch with his fingers, then looked blearily at them and sighed: 'Thanksh goodnesh! It'sh only blood.'

296. A drunk staggered across the road from the pub and into the 'chippy'. 'Could I have Rocky II?' he asked, spilling beer fumes over the counter.

66

'How many times do I have to tell you this week that this is a chip shop? The video shop is next door!' said the angry owner.

Next night the same thing was repeated, except that the drunk's request was for Psycho.

The following night, sure enough, the drunk staggered in again. 'What is it this time?' asked the owner. 'The Sound of Music?'

'Could I have chips with peas?' asked the drunk.

'At last,' thought the chip shop owner, 'we've broken through.' He dished out the chips and peas and wrapped them up carefully for the drunk. 'Will there be anything else?' he asked.

The drunk swayed on his feet. 'Oh, yes,' he said. 'And A Fish Called Wanda.'

297. The drunk came tottering out of a pub and found a man selling tortoises.

'How much are they?' asked the drunk.

'Only £10 each,' replied the seller.

'I'll take one,' said the drunk, and after he paid for the tortoise he took it and staggered off.

After twenty minutes the drunk came swaying up to the tortoise seller and bought another tortoise before teetering away.

Fifteen minutes later the drunk returned to the tortoise seller again. 'You know,' he said, as he bought yet another tortoise, 'they're very expensive – but, by jove, I really love your crunchy pies!'

298. My brother joined Alcoholics Anonymous. He still drinks, but under another name.

299. 'Owing to the drought,' said the pub sign, 'beer will be served at full strength.'

300. Farmer Smith made his chickens drink lots of whisky. He was hoping that they would lay Scotch eggs.

301. 'Why are you putting starch in your vodka?'
'Because I want a stiff drink.'

302. Father of a large family: 'If God didn't want me to have any more children he wouldn't let me drink on Saturday nights.'

303. Two nuns from the local convent found it necessary to make a visit to town to do a little late shopping for essential items. Arriving at the superstore they found that there was nowhere to park their red Mini as the car park was completely full. It was decided that one nun should go in to do the shopping whilst the other drove around until she could return to pick up her friend.

The shopping done, the first nun stood near the main road, eyes straining to meet up with her friend. Just then a man was about to pass when the nun with the shopping stopped him.

'Excuse me,' she said, 'but have you seen a nun in a red Mini?'

'Not since I took the pledge,' she was told.

304. Timothy was on holiday in Ireland and was staying at a small country inn. One evening in the bar he was amazed by the following conversation.

'That's a beautiful hat you've got there,' said an old man to a young fellow who was standing next to him at the bar. 'Where did you buy it?'

'At O'Grady's,' replied the young man.

'Why, I go there myself!' commented the old man. 'You must be from around these parts, then?'

'Aye. From Murphy Street.'

'Gracious!' exclaimed the old man. 'I live there, too!'

'Quite amazing,' commented Timothy to the barman, 'that those two folk over there live in the same street and have only just met.'

'Don't you believe it!' said the barman. 'They're

actually father and son but they're always too drunk to recognize each other.'

305. I was on holiday in Scotland and the day was so beautiful and hot that I decided to call into the pub.

'Could I have a pint of beer, landlord?' I asked.

The landlord gave a smile, pulled the beer and took the fiver I had offered him. It isn't often that I check my change but perhaps through being in a strange place I decided to do that. I smiled as I called the landlord over. 'Excuse me,' I said, 'but you've only charged me 15p for this pint of beer.'

'Oh, yes,' said the landlord. 'There's no mistake. My beer has been priced at 15p since the beginning of the year.'

I shook my head in disbelief and looked across the room where a group of locals sat playing dominoes. Funnily enough none of them were drinking beer. I wandered across and spoke to one of them.

'Why aren't you drinking?' I asked the man.

'Us?' He seemed to resent the intrusion. 'We're waiting for Happy Hour!'

306. A man on holiday in the USA was amazed at the way his host, a huge Texan, had everything so much larger than back home in England.

The car was as long as three English cars put together; the bedrooms were big enough to play a tennis match in; and the kitchen was so big it could cook enough to feed an army.

The Englishman was very impressed with all this Texan greatness, but after he had been staying in his host's gigantic house for about a week he began to drink even more than he normally did back in England.

One night, after getting particularly drunk, the Englishman fell into his host's swimming pool. When the servants rushed to rescue him they found him screaming: 'Don't flush it! Don't flush it!'

307. The car was racing along the motorway at well over a hundred miles per hour when it was forced to stop by a police car.

'You were exceeding the speed limit, sir,' said a policeman. 'Would you mind blowing into this breathalyser to see if you are fit to continue your journey?'

'But I'm in a great hurry,' replied the middle-aged male driver. 'I'm perfectly fit to drive. Can't you just give me a speeding ticket and let me continue on my journey? My wife and six year old daughter are desperately trying to get to a party on time.'

'I'm afraid I must insist on you blowing into the breathalyser, sir,' persisted the policeman.

'But I'm perfectly capable of driving,' said the man. 'Look, try out your breathalyser on my young daughter – the thing may not even be working properly.'

The policeman agreed to this suggestion and the man's six year old daughter blew into the breathalyser. To the policeman's surprise, the breathalyser turned green. He admitted to the man that it must be faulty, hurriedly wrote out a speeding ticket and let the man continue on his journey.

'I told you it would be a good idea,' said the man to his wife after they had travelled a few miles.

'Yes,' agreed his wife. 'Giving our daughter a glass of rum before we set off was one of the best ideas you've had yet.'

308. Customer: 'Can you give me something long, cold and half full of vodka?'

Waiter: 'How about my wife?'

309. A motorist, a stranger to the neighbourhood, went into a village pub late one evening and said to the landlord: 'Is there a large black dog in this village that wears a white collar?'

The publican pondered for a moment and then said: 'I cannot recollect any such animal.'

'Oh dear,' muttered the motorist, 'then I must have run over the vicar!'

310. The pretty young girl coming home by car late at night after visiting her boyfriend's house was stopped by a policeman and asked to take a breath test.

The girl blew into the breathalyser and it instantly changed colour.

'Hmmm,' said the policeman. 'You've had a stiff one tonight miss.

'My God!' exclaimed the girl. 'Does that show, too?'

311. One Red Indian stayed indoors all day drinking tea. His friends worried about him and when he had not been seen for more than a week, his friends called on him and found him drowned in his own tea pee.

ENTERTAINMENTS

312. A man wanted to enter a nightclub but was pulled up by the bouncer. 'You can't come in,' said the bouncer, 'you aren't wearing a tie.'

The disappointed man eagerly wanted to enter the club but only blamed himself for not figuring it out beforehand. With a sinking feeling and stooped shoulders he was making his way back to his car when he had a brainwave. Opening the boot he brought out his jump leads and carefully draped them around his neck to resemble a tie. 'I hope they work' he thought as he made his way back to the club.

The same bouncer was there blocking the door when the customer made his second attempt. 'Look,' said the man, looking up into the bouncer's flat face. 'I know that these are jump leads and not a tie, but could you make an exception for once?'

'All right,' said the bouncer. 'In you go, but don't start anything!'

313. The nightclub dance floor was so crowded that when one young girl fainted she had to finish the dance before she could fall down.

314. The man in the front row of the cinema was making groaning noises very loudly during a tender love scene on the screen.

'Shut up!' hissed the audience around him, but still the man continued making horrible noises.

Eventually the manager was called and he marched down the aisle until he came to the noisy man.

'Get up!' demanded the manager.

'Ooooooh!' Aaaaaaaaargh!' shouted the man, in reply.

'Where are you from?' asked the manager.

'F . . . fr . . . . . .' groaned the man, '. . . from th . . . the balcony.'

315. Just at the climax of an epic film an old man started grubbing around on the floor under the seats.

'What on earth are you doing?' the understandably irritated woman next to him rasped in a low voice.

'Trying to find my toffee,' said the man.

'Can't you leave it till the end? You are ruining the film,' snapped the woman.

'No!' croaked the old boy, 'It's got my false teeth stuck in it!'

316. A young man was sitting in the cinema when a very fat lady got up during the interval and stepped painfully on his toes while squeezing past him into the aisle.

A short time later, the same fat lady returned, carrying an ice cream and a large packet of popcorn.

'Did I tread on your toes, young man?' she asked.

'I'm afraid you did. And you didn't apologise.'

'Good,' snapped the woman. 'Then this *is* my row.'

317. A man went to see a jungle film and during the interval was surprised to see that seated next to him was a woman with a gorilla occupying the next seat. He could hardly believe his eyes and, seeing that he was so startled, the woman said: 'Oh, don't be alarmed. He liked the book, so he had to see the film.'

318. I once went to a cinema and watched a mad, passionate scene that lasted for almost half an hour – then I had to stop looking at the back row and watch the film.

319. The young girl was complaining to one of her friends: 'It was terrible! I had to change my seat five times at the cinema last night.'

'Why?' asked her friend. 'Did some chap bother you?'

'Yes – eventually.'

320. In a cinema a forward young man put his hand on a girl's leg and she slapped it away; then he put it on her knee and she did not appear to mind so much this time, so he got bolder and moved his hand up her thigh and again she slapped it away, with the remark: 'You're wasting your time; I am Picasso's daughter and what you're after is under my arm!'

321. Art Critic 1: 'I think the neo-Plasticism of the abstract design proves the mystical, metaphysical and non-humanistic approach to the objective concept of abstraction.'

Art Critic 2: 'Yes, you have a point there! In fact, it's

obvious even from a casual glance that this painting was created by paranoiac-critical activity, brought about by spontaneous dynamic sensations, sometimes made by somnambulistically inclined campanologists, who create a picture of transcendental non-curvilinear and curvilinear objects expressing subjective feelings in a cubistic manner.'

Art Critic 3: 'I fully agree with you both – it's a rubbishy painting.'

322. Jane: 'This modern art is so difficult to understand.'

Susan: 'Why? It's simple: if you can walk around it then it must be a sculpture, and if they've hung it on the wall then it can only be a picture.'

323. Van Gogh: 'My dear, please take this ear as a token of my affection for you.'

Woman: 'Th . . . thank you.'

Van Gogh: 'Pardon?'

324. A woman said to an author at a literary gathering: 'I've been making my sides ache over your latest book.'

The author was delighted: 'Oh, really?' he said. 'Did you find it very amusing?'

'No,' she replied. 'The fact is I took it to bed and fell asleep on top of it.'

325. An aspiring author sent a manuscript to an editor with a letter in which he stated: 'The characters in this story are purely fictional and bear no resemblance to any person, living or dead.'

A few days later the manuscript was returned with a brief note which read: 'That's what's wrong with it.'

326. Writer: 'I took up writing full-time about a year ago.'

Friend: 'Have you sold anything?'

Writer: 'Yes – my TV, all the furniture, the carpets, the house . . .'

327. The best selling author was being interviewed about his career.

'It seemed to me, after fifteen years of full-time writing, that I was absolutely hopeless and had no talent at all for writing.'

'So what did you do?' asked the interviewer. 'Decide to give up writing?'

'Oh, no!' replied the author. 'By that time I was far too famous.'

328. One day William Shakespeare was finding it difficult to concentrate on his writing work. Inspiration seemed to have deserted him.

Then, as he sat gnawing his pencil, he glanced at it and suddenly creative thoughts rushed into his head and he began to write: '2B or not 2B . . .'

329. The liberated father was telling his small son a bedtime story: 'And in those olden times there were lots of wicked dragons about – large creatures which snorted fire from their nostrils. One day, one of these creatures captured the beautiful daughter of the King.

'But there was a brave and bold knight who, on hearing of the plight of the princess, rapidly donned his armour and galloped off on his horse to rescue her.

'After a long and bloody battle, the knight finally slayed the dragon and rescued the princess and took her back to the King's castle.

'"You have done excellent work, knight, and have demonstrated your bravery and courage to the whole nation. I should be proud if you would take my daughter's hand in marriage – or become the husband of any of my other offspring."

'Now, son, think carefully. Whom do you think the knight married?'

'The princess he rescued, of course,' replied his small son.

'No, you're wrong,' said the father. 'He married the King's son. After all, what else can you expect in a fairy story?'

330. Two men in a saloon were playing cards. One of them thumped the table happily with his fist and cried: 'I win!'

'What have you got?' asked the other cowboy.

'Four aces.'

'I'm afraid you don't win.'

'That's almost impossible,' declared the first man. 'What cards have you got?'

'Two nines and a loaded gun.'

'Oh,' said the first man. 'You win. But how come you're so lucky?'

331. Claude: 'Philip! Stop cheating with the cards.'

Philip: 'How do you know I'm cheating?'

Claude: 'Because you're not playing the hand I dealt you.'

332. Simon: 'I took my wife to the theatre last night – but we only saw the first Act and then had to leave.'

Sally: 'Why was that?'

Simon: 'Well, on the programme it said: "Act Two: Two days later" – and we couldn't stay in the theatre that long.'

333. The Concert Secretary of the Social Club stood beside the doorman awaiting the arrival of the Artistes. The door opened and in walked a man carrying equipment.

'You're not a hypnotist, are you?' he asked. 'If so, you can go somewhere else. You won't be welcome here.'

'I'm a singer,' explained the man. 'Why? What's wrong?'

'We had a hypnotist last week,' explained the Concert Secretary 'and he got twenty people on stage. He had just got them under when he tripped over his microphone wire.'

'And . . . ?' asked a now inquisitive Artiste.

'He said SH**, and we've been cleaning it up all week,' replied the official.

334. A ventriloquist's act was going down better than he thought it would have done, perhaps due to the fact that he had chosen one particular customer at the front of the audience to take the mickey from. Throughout the act the customer took it all in good part as the ventriloquist poured out cheap jibes at his expense. But then, all of a sudden, he jumped from his seat and started shouting.

The ventriloquist, fearing that if he upset the customers he might lose his job, thought he had better apologise, which he duly did.

However, the man got more agitated and shouted to him: 'I'm not talking to you. I'm talking to that little swine on your knee!'

335. A magician on board a cruise ship used to do amazing tricks every night in the cabaret spot – but the captain's pet parrot always used to shout 'Phoney, phoney!' at the end of the magician's act.

Then one day the ship hit an iceberg and sank, but the magician and the parrot managed to cling to a piece of wood and float clear of the sinking ship.

After a few minutes of floating, the parrot turned an inquisitive beak to the magician and said: 'OK, genius. What have you done with the ship?'

336. Compère comments:

'This evening, one of the beautiful chorus girls was

hammering on my dressing-room door for more than fifty minutes . . . but I wouldn't let her out.'

'After such a warm reception I can hardly wait to hear myself speak.'

'The only thing wrong with the show tonight is that the seats face the stage.'

'Our next guest is that famous gossip columnist who, when she dies, will attract hundreds of thousands of people to her funeral – just to make quite sure she really *is* dead.'

To heckler: 'There's a bus leaving after the show, sir – please be under it.'

337. The ageing actor was trying to chat up the gorgeous young girl.
'Don't you recognize me?' he asked. She shook her head.
'But I'm quite well known in the movies,' he continued.
'Oh!' she said, her eyes lighting up. 'Where do you usually sit?'

338. I thought the television programmes had improved tremendously – until my wife told me I'd been watching the fish tank she'd swapped for the TV.

339. Quizmaster: 'On which side was the Pope shot?'
Contestant: 'I think it was ITV.'

340. Timothy Tattle, a rather shy middle-aged man, got lost in the back streets of Soho one day. Suddenly a furtive looking man in a shabby raincoat slipped out of a shop doorway and sidled up to Timothy.
'Want to buy any pornographic pictures?' asked the

man.

'Certainly not!' replied Timothy. 'I don't even own a pornograph.'

341. I knew my uncle was a true opera lover when I caught him outside the bathroom door where our beautiful au pair was having a bath. She was singing an excerpt from *Der Rosenkavalier* and my uncle didn't peer through the keyhole to look at her gorgeous naked body – but put his ear to it!

342. The London Philharmonic Orchestra were playing the Bermuda Rhapsody when the triangle player disappeared.

343. When Cyril visited the house of his least favourite nephew he was forced to endure the latter's not very good piano playing.

After he had finished his performance the nephew asked: 'How was that?'

'You should be on TV,' replied Cyril.

'You mean I'm that good?' said the nephew, clearly delighted.

'No. But if you were on TV at least I could turn you off.'

344. What do you get when you drop a grand piano down a coal mine? A flat miner.

345. 'There's a fish in my grand piano.'

'That's all right – it's only a piano tuna.'

346. I learnt to play the piano in ten easy lessons. It was the first ninety that were difficult.

347. Piano tuner: 'Good morning, sir, I've come to tune your piano.'

Mr Smith: 'But I didn't ask for a piano tuner.'
Piano tuner: 'I know sir, but your neighbours did.'

348. A band was playing in the street and one of their number was collecting. Approaching one house he opened the gate, walked up the path and knocked. The door was opened by an old lady to whom he said, 'We're the Accrington Stanley and District Prize Band and we're collecting.'

'Eh?' she said.

So he repeated: 'We're the Accrington Stanley and District Prize Band and we're collecting.'

'It's no use,' she said, 'I can't hear a word you're saying.'

Thereupon the man turned on his heel saying under his breath: 'To hell with yer.'

Quick as a flash she replied: 'And to hell with the Accrington Stanley and District Prize Band.'

349. 'Will the band play anything I request?'

'Certainly, sir.'

'Then tell them to play dominoes.'

350. The orchestra had just finished playing a delightful little number called 'Tuning Up', and the audience were eagerly awaiting the arrival of the world-famous conductor, Igor Driftwood.

The tension mounted as the brilliant conductor delayed his entrance until the last possible moment – then he appeared and the audience went wild with delight, clapping and jumping up and down in ecstasy at being so privileged to see a man of such sheer genius.

Igor made his way to the conductor's platform to even greater cheers. He tapped his music stand, and all was silence.

Then he looked down at the music stand and said: 'Er . . . excuse me, but what are these five lines and all the black dots and funny squiggles on them?'

351. A friend of mine knew his son was going to be an actor when he caught him opening the fridge and taking a bow when the little light came on.

352. The Hollywood actor had to look seedy for his latest role and the make-up man gave him a moustache that had been made from the hair from a dog's leg. It made him look seedy all right – but whenever he walked past a lamp post the moustache curled upwards.

353. The Hollywood props department manager answered his phone only to hear the producer bawl at him: 'Why haven't you got me the full-scale mock up of the inside of the *Titanic* like I asked for this morning? How the hell do you expect me to make a film about King Canute without the props I ask for?'

'But . . but . . .' stammered the props manager.

'Don't "but . . . but . . ." me!' roared the producer. 'Nobody on this film seems to care about accuracy and realism except me. Now, get me those props or . . .'

'But if you keep shouting all the time,' soothed the props manager, 'you'll get ulcers and . . .'

'I don't *get* ulcers!' roared the producer. 'I *give* them!'

354. Artist: 'You know, you're the first model I've ever made love to.'

Nude model: 'I don't believe you. I bet you say that to all the models you've painted. How many have you had?'

Artist: 'Well, there was a bowl of fruit, a dog, the watermill . . .'

FACTORIES & TRADE

355. A woman remarked to her husband who was lying in bed with his feet on the pillow and his head at the foot of the bed: 'I can't understand what's come over you, Jack, since you started work at the sardine factory.'

356. Foreman: 'Can you brew a good cup of tea?'
Applicant: 'Yes.'
Foreman: 'Can you drive a stacker truck?'
Applicant: Why? Is it a big teapot?'

357. Two tradesmen of the town met. 'Trade's bad,' said one man. 'I heard that your factory burned down today.'
'Hush!' said the second. 'It's tomorrow!'

358. A trade union leader went to his doctor for help in getting to sleep. The doctor was reluctant to put the union leader on sleeping pills until other remedies had been tried and so he asked the man to lie quite still in bed at night and count sheep.
The trade union leader did this, but by the time he'd counted the twenty-seventh sheep they'd all gone on strike for shorter hours and lower fences.

359. A young lad started as an apprentice in a large works and after a time was put on a machine making small parts. One day the foreman asked him how the work was turning out and the lad answered: 'Oh, near enough.'

The foreman then and there gave a brief lecture on performing a job so that the work was 'dead right'; 'near enough' was not good enough.

A few days later he saw the lad again and said: 'How are things turning out now?'

'Dead right,' replied the boy.

'Good,' said the foreman. 'That's near enough.'

FAMILIES

360. Rachel: 'Yours is a big family, isn't it? Aren't you a twin?'

Maria: 'Yes.'

Rachel: 'Can they tell you apart?'

Maria: 'I expect so.'

Rachel: 'How?'

Maria: 'Because Fred has a moustache!'

361. Eighteen-year-old son: 'Dad?'

Father: 'Yes, son?'

Eighteen-year-old son: 'Did you ever make love when you were my age?'

Father: 'Yes, son. And let it be a horrible warning to you.'

Eighteen-year-old son: 'Why, what happened?'

Father: 'I ended up marrying your mother.'

362. For eleven years Duncan had put up with the fat, interfering old woman. Now he could stand it no longer.

'She's got to go,' he said to his wife. 'I can't stand your mother another minute!'

'My mother!' exclaimed Duncan's wife. 'I thought she was *your* mother!'

363. Sarah was walking along pushing her new baby in its pram when an old friend approached, looked into the pram and said: 'My, he's beautiful. He looks just like his father.'

'I know,' said Sarah. 'It's a pity he doesn't look more like my husband.'

364. A small boy was peering through a hole in the fence of a nudist colony. His friend, Paul, came up to him and asked: 'Tim, what can you see? Are they men or women in there?'

'I don't really know,' replied Tim. 'None of them have got any clothes on.'

365. Little girl: 'Mummy, do all fairy tales begin with 'Once upon a time . . . ?'

Mother: 'No, darling. Some start with, "Sorry I'm so late dear, I was detained at the office."'

366. Mavis: 'My children are terrible. They climb all over everywhere and never give me a moment's peace. How do you keep so calm?'

Jane: 'It's all due to the wonders of a play pen. I sit inside it and the kids can't get me!'

367. A Society hostess was giving a cocktail party and to her great surprise, in the midst of the proceedings, her young son and daughter, completely naked, entered the room, passed among the guests and then left. Of course, the guests pretended not to notice them, but as soon as she could excuse herself, the mother hurried upstairs to the children and said: 'My dears, whatever did you think you were doing just now?'

'Oh, Mummy,' they replied, 'we went into your room and found a tube with "Vanishing Cream" on it. So we smeared ourselves all over, went downstairs, and no one could see us!'

368. Mr Smith was taking his five-year-old son for a walk when a beggar came up to him and said: 'Can you help me, sir? I haven't had a bite for a whole week.'

Before Mr Smith could say anything, his son had bitten the beggar.

369. The little boy and girl were being bathed together and Sophie inquired of her brother: 'What is that?'

'That's mine,' said Henry.

'Can I play with it?' questioned Sophie.

'No!' retorted Henry '— just because you've broken yours already!'

370. Small daughter: 'Mummy, how many more days is it before Christmas?'

Mother: 'Not many. Why do you ask?'

Small daughter: 'I just wondered if it's near enough for me to start being a good little girl.'

371. Proud father: 'Our household represents the whole United Kingdom. I am English, my wife's Irish, the nurse comes from Scotland, and the baby wails.'

372. A middle-aged woman clambered on to a bus with three sets of twins trailing behind her. When they were all seated in the bus, the conductor asked her: 'Do you always get twins?'

'Oh, no!' replied the woman. 'Hundreds of times we don't get anything.'

373. Sally: 'Mummy, do you like baked apples?'

Mother: 'Yes, of course. Don't you remember, we had them last week. Why do you ask?'

Sally: 'Because the orchard is on fire.'

374. Five-year-old Lionel: 'Mummy, can I go in the sea?'

Mother: 'Not today, Lionel. Maybe tomorrow. The

sea is far too rough and choppy now.'

Lionel: 'But Daddy is in the sea swimming.'

Mother: 'I know, dear. But he's got lots of life assurance cover.'

375. The little girl had been taken to the supermarket by her mother but had somehow managed to get lost near the tinned food section.

'Excuse me,' asked the little girl of another customer. 'Have you seen a mother walking along pushing a shopping trolley without a girl like me?'

376. A middle-aged woman was on her way to the shops when she saw a small boy leaning against a wall, smoking a cigar and swigging a bottle of whisky. The woman was appalled at this and rushed over to the boy and demanded: 'Why aren't you at school at this time of day?'

'At school?' queried the boy, taking another swig at the bottle. 'Hell, lady, I'm only four years old!'

377. Simon had been warned that he must be on his best behaviour when his wealthy aunt arrived for a brief holiday visit.

It was at tea during the first day of her stay that Simon kept looking at his aunt then, when the meal was almost finished, he asked: 'Auntie, when are you going to do your trick?'

'What trick is that, dear?' she inquired.

'Well,' began Simon, 'Daddy says you can drink like a fish.'

378. Mr and Mrs O'Reilly had been trying for a son for many, many years and, after eleven daughters they were eventually rewarded with a son.

'Who does he look like?' asked a friend, visiting the maternity hospital to see Mrs O'Reilly.

'We don't know,' replied Mrs O'Reilly. 'We haven't looked at his face yet.'

379. Angela's mother was looking in the mirror and plucking out the few grey hairs which she found in her head.

'Mummy, why do you have some grey hair?' inquired Angela.

'Probably because you're such a naughty girl and cause me so much worry.'

'Oh!' said Angela. 'You must have been a devil towards grandmother.'

380. The two little girls were busy boasting to each other about how great their respective fathers were.

'*My* father had lunch with Shakespeare yesterday,' said Sally.

'But Shakespeare is dead,' commented Clare.

'Oh,' replied Sally, unperturbed. 'No wonder dad said he was quiet.'

381. A nice little girl was taken by her father to a séance which was being held at the home of a friend of his who worked in the same factory.

When they arrived at the house the séance had just started and the medium asked the little girl if there was anyone she would like to speak to.

'I'd very much like to talk to my old grandmother,' replied the little girl in a soft voice.

'Certainly, my dear,' said the medium, and shortly afterwards went into a trance. Suddenly the medium began to talk in a strange voice – the voice saying: 'This is your old grandmother speaking from Heaven – a glorious place high in the skies. Would you like to ask me anything, my child?'

'Yes, grandmother,' said the little girl. 'Why are you speaking from Heaven when you're not even dead yet?'

382. Mandy was growing very rapidly and her mother was very proud of this and so wrote and told Mandy's grandmother that Mandy had grown another foot since the last time she had seen her.

Almost by return post, Mandy's grandmother sent her another sock.

383. 'Mummy, mummy! Where are you?' cried the little boy on the promenade at Bournemouth.

'You poor little boy,' said an elderly lady. 'Come with me and I'll get you an ice cream and then we'll go and look for your mummy and if we still can't find her I'll take you to the nice man who rents out the beach huts and he'll get the police to look for your mummy.'

'I know where your mummy is,' said a small girl. 'She's . . .'

'Shush!' whispered the little boy. 'I know where she is, too, but this way I've already had two free ice creams this morning from other people before we found my mother – don't be mean and stop me getting a third one!'

384. A father who had one leg shorter than the other and thus walked with a slight limp, had a son who stuttered.

One day the son said: 'D-d-dad, I've g-g-got a go-good idea. Why don't you wa-walk with one f-foot in the gutter? Then yo-our limp wo-wouldn't be noticed.'

'Good idea, son,' said his father, 'I'll try it.' So he did and was knocked down by a car.

The son visited him in hospital. 'So s-sorry about yo-your accident, D-dad,' he said.

'That's all right,' said the father, 'but while I've been here I've been thinking and I've got an idea about your stutter.'

'What's that, D-dad?' asked the son.

'Keep your blinking mouth shut,' came the reply.

385. Brian's mother and father had told him about the facts of life, but when it came to telling their younger son, only seven years old, they were too embarrassed.

'Brian, will you tell John about the birds and the bees?' pleaded Brian's father.

Brian agreed and that night Brian asked John: 'Do you know what mum and dad do at night in bed?'

'Of course I know,' replied John.

'Well,' said Brian, 'it's the same with birds and bees.'

386. A woman got on a bus with seven children. The conductor asked: 'Are these all yours, lady? Or is it a picnic?'

'They're all mine,' came the reply. 'And it's no picnic!'

387. A rather fastidious man was sitting in a bus opposite a woman who was accompanied by a small boy who kept on sniffing. At last the chap could stand it no longer, so he said to the woman: 'Hasn't this boy got a handkerchief?'

'Yes, he has,' came the reply, 'but he's not lending it to you.'

388. Samantha was a six-year-old who liked to exaggerate almost everything she saw or did.

One day she was looking out of the window when she called to her mother: 'Mummy, Mummy! Come quickly! There's a lion walking in the road outside our house!'

Samantha's mother looked out of the window, but could only see a small ginger cat.

'Samantha! You're lying again!' she scolded. 'Go upstairs to your room immediately and pray to God for forgiveness for being such a naughty little girl – and beg him to stop you from telling so many lies.'

Samantha ran up to her room, sobbing. A short time later she came down to her mother and said: 'I've prayed to God like you said, Mummy, and He said that *He* thought the ginger cat looked rather like a lion too.'

389. A woman was telling her married daughter that

the cold weather was bad for her rheumatism. Her little granddaughter was present and overheard the conversation. She didn't say anything then, but that night when she went to bed she knew what she was going to do. After she had said her usual prayers she concluded by saying: 'And please, God, make it hot for Grandma!'

390. A mother, fearing that she might have caught a cold, took a little whisky and hot water as a precaution. As she tucked up her little daughter in bed shortly afterwards, a look of reproach came over the little one's face. 'Oh, Mummy!' she said. 'You've been using Daddy's scent.'

391. Father to son: 'Please don't pester me with so many questions. I've answered you about a hundred times today already. What do you think would have happened if I had asked my father so many questions?'

'Well, Dad,' replied the boy. 'Perhaps you might have learnt how to answer some of mine.'

392. In a rush to get on the bus a little boy was badly jostled by a man who was trying to get out. He complained to his father: 'Father,' he said, 'that man ought to be punished. He trod on my foot and hurt me.'

His father replied: 'He's already been punished, my son. I've got his wallet.'

393. 'Granny, can you do an impression of a frog?' asked three-year-old Sarah.

'Why?' asked Granny.

'Because,' replied Sarah, 'I heard mummy and daddy talking and they said we'd get a small fortune when you croak.'

394. 'Mummy, there's a man with a bill at the door.'

'Don't be silly, dear. It must be a duck with a hat on.'

395. After waiting impatiently for some time, a little girl became old enough to join the Brownies. She returned from the interview bubbling over with excitement and said: 'Mummy, the lady says that if I go along next week she will unroll me!'

396. Two little boys were looking out of the window when they saw a lorry drive past loaded with turf.

'That's what I shall do when I'm rich,' said one of the little boys. 'I'll send my grass away to be cut, too.'

397. A boy said to another: 'If you're at the seaside and you want to teach a girl to swim, how do you go about it?'

Replied the other: 'You take her gently by the hand and lead her down to the water's edge and gradually wade out with her until you're about waist deep and then you let her fall gracefully forward with your hand cupped under her chin, at the same time she strikes out with her arms in a firm circular motion.'

'Coo,' the first boy said, 'you seem to know all about it. But what if it's your sister?'

'Oh,' came the reply, 'you just shove her in.'

398. A little girl was going to a party and her mother told her to be a good little girl and to remember, when she was leaving, to thank her hostess.

When she arrived home, the mother asked her if she had thanked her hostess and the little girl replied: 'No, the girl in front of me did and the lady said "Don't mention it" – so I didn't.'

399. A young woman was asked by a friend what name she was going to give to her new baby son. 'Well,' she replied, 'we thought of calling him David.'

'Oh,' the other retorted, 'I shouldn't. Every Tom, Dick and Harry is called David, nowadays.'

400. Her first child was born with callouses on his hands. It was through trying to hold on until after the wedding.

401. My husband was a war baby. When he was born his parents took one look at him and started fighting.

402. Mrs Jones shouted at her small son, who was outside in the rain: 'What are you doing out there in the rain?'

'Getting wet,' replied her small son.

403. 'Mummy, mummy! The milkman's at the door. Have you got the money – or shall I go out and play?'

404. Mother: 'Why are you scratching yourself?'

Three-year-old Anna: 'Because only I know where I itch.'

405. I learned to swim at a very early age. When I was three my parents used to row me out to sea in a little boat until they got about a mile or so away from the shore, then I had to swim back. I quite liked the swim – it was getting out of the sack that was difficult.

406. Mother: 'Where did all the jam tarts go? I only made them an hour ago and I told you not to eat them all – now there's only one left.'

Fat son: 'So? I did what you said. I didn't eat them *all* – I left one.'

407. 'Bernard!' screamed Bernard's mother. 'Why did you fall in that mud wearing your new trousers?'

'Because,' replied Bernard, 'there wasn't time to take them off.'

408. Man: 'I cured my son of biting his nails.'

Friend: 'Oh, how?'
Man: 'Knocked all his teeth out.'

409. A father had invited a business friend to lunch and when the joint was put on the table, the young son of the house exclaimed: 'Why, it's roast beef.'

'What did you expect then?' asked his mother.

'Well,' replied the boy. 'I heard Daddy say last night that he was bringing a proper mutton head home for lunch today.'

410. 'Dad. Now that I'm 14 can I wear silk stockings and a brassiere?'

'No, Derek, you can't!'

411. The young son of the house ran into the room where his mother was sitting and said, 'Come at once, there's a man in the kitchen kissing the au pair girl.'

As his mother rose to look into the matter he cried out gleefully: 'April Fool, it's only father!'

412. Two little girls were talking. One said: 'It's my Mummy's birthday today, she's twenty-six.'

'Golly,' replied the other. 'She's getting old.'

'She sure is,' said the first little girl. 'And, do you know, she can still ride a bicycle.'

413. Starting research for a book in which it was planned to show the difficult conditions resulting from large families, a sociologist interviewed the mother of thirteen children. After obtaining the information regarding the children's ages, the family income and other relative matters, he asked: 'Do you think that all children deserve the full, impartial love of a mother?'

'Of course,' she replied.

'Well, which of your children do you love the most?' he asked, hoping to catch her out in a contradiction.

'The one who is sick, until he gets well, and the one

who is away, until he returns home,' she answered.

414. A young man had a good win on the football pools and shortly after he had received the cheque he said to his father: 'Oh, look, Dad, you've always been decent to me, so here's a pound.'

The father took the money, thought for a moment and then said: 'Well, thanks, son. Now, do you mind if I give you a little bit of advice?'

'Of course not, Dad,' replied the other.

'Well, son,' went on the father, 'when you're a little older and get a girl and think of settling down, don't do what your mother and I did. You get married properly.'

The son was staggered. 'But Dad,' he said, 'do you realize what you've just said? That makes me a bastard!'

'I know, son,' replied the father, 'and a mean one at that!'

415. John: 'Mummy, Barry has just broken a pane of glass in the greenhouse.'

Mother: 'How did he do that?'

John: 'I threw my cricket bat at him and he ducked.'

416. A little boy had just returned home after an outing with his father.

'Well, dear, how did you like the zoo?' asked the boy's mother.

'Oh, it was great!' replied the boy. 'And Dad liked it too – especially when one of the animals came racing home at thirty to one.'

417. He's just like his father.'

'I know – bald, sleepy and uneducated.'

418. My young daughter's singing is rather like a quiz show – Maim That Tune.

419. It has been said that children brighten a home. I suppose that's because they never turn any of the lights off.

420. My young son took his nose apart this morning. He wanted to see what made it run.

421. Mother: 'Why have you dragged your bed out into the woodshed?'
Samantha: 'Because I want to sleep like a log.'

422. The extremely wealthy man (who had inherited his wealth) bought his son a slum. He wanted him to have everything he missed when he was a child.

423. Just before Christmas Fred tried to cross an octopus with a chicken – so his family could have a leg each.

424. Lady Bloggis: 'We're having a party at the weekend to celebrate my daughter's coming out.'
Mavis Grunter-Tottle: 'How long was she inside – and what did she do?'

425. 'Mummy. What's that wrinkled thing grandad keeps taking out?'
'That will be grandma.'

426. Father to small boy: 'How many millions of times have I told you not to exaggerate?'

427. I have a friend called Tuesday. I know it's unusual but when he was born his parents thought they'd call it a day.

428. My neighbour asked me to drive him to the airport where he wanted to greet his brother who had been in America for the last 30 years, in fact since they were both boys.

'Will he know you?' I asked him.

'He should do,' said my neighbour. '*I* haven't been away.'

429. My Aunt Gladys took up body building recently. She did it so well that now she's my uncle.

430. Jim: 'My old uncle has one foot in the grate.'

Bob: 'Don't you mean he's got one foot in the grave?'

Jim: 'No. He wants to be cremated.'

431. My mother-in-law believes in free speech – particularly long distance phone calls from our house.

432. I had a relation who was so mean about money that he broke into his neighbour's house to gas himself.

433. The meanest man in the world was the one who fired a revolver on Christmas Eve outside the door, then came in and told his children that Father Christmas had committed suicide.

434. My brother is so mean. Before I got married he promised us a food mixer as a wedding present, and I was so surprised at his unexpected generosity. On the wedding day, however, he handed me his carefully wrapped food mixer – a wooden spoon!

435. One woman paid a genealogist a thousand pounds to trace her family tree – then she had to pay another thousand to have it hushed up.

436. The warm summer air drifted into the Red Lion as Fred and his boozing pal Alf sat by the open window to take advantage of the afternoon breeze. Most things had been discussed whilst downing the landlord's best bitter, from the state of the country, the doping of race horses, to the state of education.

'They don't teach them the same as they did when we went to school,' said Fred.

'I blame the teachers,' offered Alf. 'I think that I have the thickest lad in this town,' he went on.

'He can't be as thick as my boy. Dense isn't the word,' said Fred.

'Look,' Alf said. 'They will be coming out of school any minute. Let's call them in and ask them something daft. See if they swallow it!'

The church clock struck the hour and out poured those little bundles of noisy energy called school children. Alf's son was the first to appear in front of the pub window, so his father called him in. He pushed a 50p piece into the lad's hand and told him to go to the television shop in the High Street and buy a television. Without asking anything the lad took the money and went from the pub.

Fred peered through the window until he caught sight of his son and called for him to come in. In the meantime, Alf discussed with his friend that his lad was as thick as he said and Fred agreed.

Fred's son came through the door and stood before his father, wondering what he had done wrong. 'See this?' Fred asked him, producing a pound coin. 'I want you to take this because I'm going to ask you to do something.' The boy looked blank but accepted the gift.

'I want you,' went on Fred, 'to run down to the British Legion and see if I'm in!'

The boy scratched his head and made for the door, leaving the two adults doubled up with laughter.

Opening the door he saw Alf's son sitting on the steps of the pub.

'I think my dad is thick!' said the lad. 'He's just given me 50p to buy a TV and he didn't say what make he wanted.'

'He's not as thick as my dad,' said his friend. 'My dad has given me a pound to see if he's in the British Legion – and he could have used the pub's telephone for less than that!'

FORCES

437. A young Royal Air Force officer was returning to his unit late one night when his car had a puncture. As he stood by the roadside in order to change the wheel, he heard a small voice say: 'Be careful, you nearly trod on me just then.'

Looking down he saw a frog and he asked it: 'Did you speak to me just now?'

'Yes, I did,' said the frog, 'and now that you've had to stop, perhaps you'll kindly give me a lift.'

'Certainly,' said the young officer, 'as soon as I've changed this wheel. So hop in.'

The frog did so, and presently the officer drove off until he came to the establishment where he was stationed. Then, turning to the frog which was sitting in the passenger seat, he said: 'I'm afraid that I can't take you any farther as I am due back right now.'

Then the frog said: 'Now, I am not just an ordinary frog. Actually I am a policewoman and I have been changed into a frog by my wicked godmother. But if you take me into your billet and let me sleep on your pillow for one night, the spell will be broken and I shall change back.'

'Good heavens,' said the officer, 'I couldn't do that, I should get into awful trouble if anyone found out.'

'Oh, be a sport,' said the frog. 'Just think of my

predicament.'

Thus appealed to, the officer said: 'Oh, well, I'll take a chance.'

And that's the story he told the court marshal.

438. It happened during the First World War that a Staff Officer wished to be taken up to the front line, so a private in a jeep was detailed to escort him.

They started off and presently the private whispered: 'Shell hole on the left,' and the officer nodded.

Again, the private whispered: 'Old enemy trenches on the right,' and the officer whispered back: 'I see them.'

After a while another whisper: 'Barbed wire entanglements on the left,' and the officer whispered: 'Yes, I see them.'

They had been proceeding in this way for some time when the officer said: 'I say, it's very quiet, how far are we from the front line?'

'About two miles,' came the reply, again in a whisper.

'Then whatever are we whispering for?' demanded the officer.

'You needn't,' replied the private. 'I've got a sore throat.'

439. When National Service was in force in England a young man who was called up pleaded very bad eyesight and so it appeared. He failed all the usual tests and then in desperation the examiner held up a dustbin lid and said: 'Tell me, what is this?'

The fellow blinked and then said: 'Well, it's either a two bob bit or half a crown.'

Well, he was not accepted and in great glee the chap went off to celebrate with a visit to a cinema. He had not been sitting there very long when, to his horror, who should come and sit down next to him, but the examiner. They recognized each other, but, quick as a flash, the rejected conscript said: 'Am I on the right bus for Bromley?'

440. Well-chosen Bible texts are sometimes so apt in summarizing real life situations. Some years ago when a young man received his call-up papers, he replied to the War Office: 'See Luke 14:20.' This reads: 'I have married a wife and therefore I cannot come.'

The War Office aptly replied: 'See Luke 7:8.' This states: 'For I also am a man set under authority, having under me soldiers, and I say unto one, "Go" and he goeth, and to another, "Come", and he cometh.'

441. The company was on parade and the Sergeant Major asked: 'Are there any men here who are fond of music?'

Three or four responded to whom he instructed: 'Fall out and report for shifting the canteen piano.'

442. A group of soldiers were standing around talking when the Sergeant Major appeared and said: 'What's going on here?'

'Oh,' said one of the men. 'I was telling them about my dream.'

'Go on,' said the Sergeant Major, 'let's hear about it.'

'Well,' replied the other, 'I dreamt that there was a tall ladder reaching up into the sky and an angel appeared and, giving me a piece of chalk, told me to make a mark on a different rung for every sin that I had committed. So, I started off and then to my great surprise I saw you coming down for more chalk!'

443. The RAF had cut back and cut back almost to the hilt and this was causing concern among the air crews, but things came to a head one particular day when the plane was out on duty flying high with a full crew of anxious parachutists.

The pilot could feel the unease amongst the men and he was told that he should go and look at the large cardboard box in which the parachutes had been sent.

The pilot left the aircraft in the capable hands of the co-pilot and he moved through the men to the large cardboard box that had held the chutes. He slowly turned the box over and in deep black print it read: 'Opens on impact.'

444. When I was in the army I lost my rifle and had to report it. The officer said: 'That's all right. Give me your pay book and we'll stop it out of your pay. It will cost you a thousand pounds.'

I said: 'What if I lost a jeep?'

He said: 'Just the same. The money will be taken from your pay book.'

'A rocket launcher?' I timidly asked. He gave a wry smile.

I said: 'Good lord. No wonder a captain goes down with his ship!'

445. The squad were having a musketry lesson. Suddenly the sergeant in charge turned to one of the men who had not been paying strict attention and asked him: 'What is a fine sight?'

He was staggered when the fellow answered: 'Two dinners for one on the same plate.'

446. General: 'Can you tell me what a soldier must be before he can be buried with full military honours?'

Private: 'Dead, sir.'

HOLIDAYS & HOTELS

447. Hotel receptionist in Spain to Englishman: 'Are you a foreigner?'
Englishman: 'Certainly not! I'm British!'

448. I once stayed at a hotel in Venice that was so damp there were goldfish in the mousetrap!

449. Holidays in the USA make you feel good enough to return to work – and so poor that you're forced to.

450. Resident of Barbados: 'In Barbados we always have fantastic weather.'
Visiting English woman: 'Then how on earth do you start a conversation with a stranger?'

451. A holiday is something you have for two weeks that takes fifty weeks to pay for.

452. The last time I went on holiday for a fortnight it only rained twice: the first time for seven days, and the second time for a week.

453. The weather was terrible for the whole two weeks of my holiday. I didn't get brown from the sun, but from the rust caused by the rain.

454. Two little boys were paddling in the sea at Margate.
'Coo, ain't your feet dirty?' said one little boy.
'Yes,' replied the other, 'we didn't come last year.'

455. A beautiful young girl was lying, asleep, in a tiny bikini immediately below the promenade. A small boy accidentally dropped a piece of his vanilla ice-cream on her, and it landed on her naval.

The girl immediately awoke and sprang to her feet, shocked, and said: 'These seagulls must live in a flipping refrigerator!'

456. A visitor to the Mid West asked: 'Any big men ever born in this town?'

'No,' came the reply. 'Just little babies.'

457. It was on a sightseeing coach tour of New York that the Welshman turned to his companion, a boastful American, and said: 'And where do you come from?'

'From God's own country,' replied the American.

'Hmm,' said the Welshman, 'then you've got a very poor Welsh accent!'

458. Jackie: 'How was your holiday in Switzerland? Did you like the scenery?'

Sarah: 'Not really. You couldn't see much as the mountains kept getting in the way.'

459. Traveller: 'Excuse me, do you have a room for tonight?'

Hotel proprietor: 'Certainly, sir. It'll be £30 a night, or I can let you have a room for only £10 if you make your own bed.'

Traveller: 'I'll take the £10 room.'

Hotel proprietor: 'Right! I'll just go and fetch the wood, the hammer and the nails and other materials for the bed . . .'

460. Robert: 'That's the last time I stay in such a posh hotel.'

Alan: 'Why, what was wrong with it?'

Robert: 'They even made me wear a jacket and tie when I was in the sauna.'

461. I once stayed in a hotel where the walls of our room were so thin that every time I asked my wife a question I got three different answers.

462. Hugh once stayed in a hotel in Thailand where they catered for a guest's every whim.

The first night he was in his hotel room when the manager knocked on the door and called out: 'Do you have a girl in your room?'

When Hugh called back 'No!' the manager asked: 'Do you want one?'

463. A man was shown up to the room which had been offered to him in a hotel by a rather pretty chambermaid.

'Yes,' he said, 'this will suit me very well. And, may I ask, are you to be let with the room?'

'Certainly not,' she replied. 'I am to be let alone!'

464. It was a posh hotel. Room service was ex-directory.

465. A man was going away for a holiday to the West Country and mentioned the name of the place to a friend who said at once: 'Oh, I've a very great friend who lives there. If you should come across her and you might easily do so, you might remember me to her.'

'Certainly,' was the reply. 'What is her name?'

'Dummock,' said the other.

Now, the holiday maker thought to himself: 'How shall I remember that? Ah! I have it, I'll think of stomach.' (As a matter of fact he was always thinking of his stomach.) 'As it rhymes with Dummock, all should be well.'

He went off for his holiday and on his return ran into his friend and said at once: 'I'm very sorry but I didn't see anything of your friend, Miss Kelly.'

466. After a club booking in the Midlands I had a few

jars and then decided to look for some decent digs. As it happened, due to the late hour, I could only find one boarding house with a vacant sign. Pushing the door open and feeling rather tired I walked in.

'I've only got one room left,' said the man behind the desk, 'and you'll have to share with another bloke, but . . .'

'But what?' I asked.

'Watch his snoring,' I was warned. 'We've had complaints!'

Reluctantly I took the room and the morning after I was met on the stairs by the desk clerk.

'How did you get on last night?' he wanted to know.

'Smashing,' I told him. 'Before I turned in last night I leaned across and kissed him and he stayed awake all night!'

467. It was one o'clock in the morning and the manager of the hotel had just been woken by a frantic phone call from a little old lady. 'Come quickly! Oh, please come quickly!' she wailed. 'I can see a naked man from my window.'

The manager hastily dressed and rushed up to the little old lady's room. He found her pointing at a block of flats opposite her hotel bedroom – but all the manager could see was the naked top half of a young man.

'But my dear woman,' soothed the manager, 'the young man opposite is surely only preparing for bed. And how can you possibly be offended by him? The man may not be completely naked.'

'The wardrobe!' shrieked the little old lady. 'Stand on the wardrobe!'

468. Journeying in Africa, a traveller called on a friendly tribe and found to his great surprise that he knew the chief, who had been at school with him in England. Of course, the traveller was given a great welcome and he was able to stay for a few days.

The chief asked the traveller if he would like to take away something as a souvenir. Now, the chief had a fine carved wooden throne and the traveller asked if a replica of it could be made for him. The chief agreed and it was made and presented to the traveller who stored it, for the few more days that he was to remain, at the top of a large wooden pole in the grass house which the chief had placed at his disposal.

That night a great storm arose and the throne came hurtling down and smashed into a thousand pieces. Now the moral of this story is – people who live in grass houses shouldn't stow thrones.

469. The new porter at a hotel in Mexico had been given careful instructions as to how to behave with courtesy and efficiency.

'You should try and welcome each guest by name,' instructed the hotel manager.

'But how can I do that? How will I know their names?' asked the porter.

'Simple!' explained the manager. 'Each guest usually has his or her name written on their luggage.'

So the first couple to enter the hotel and be welcomed by the new porter were greeted: 'Welcome, Mr and Mrs Simulated Real Leather.'

470. A tourist in Scotland, who had been admiring the scenery, stopped as he passed through a village and asked one of the inhabitants: 'Is this a healthy place?'

'Aye, it is,' came the reply. 'There's been only one death in the last ten years, and that was the local undertaker who died of starvation.'

471. English Tourist: 'I'm on holiday but I'd like to settle here.'

Australian Immigration Officer: 'Do you have a prison record?'

English Tourist: 'I didn't think we needed them anymore!'

472. A guide was showing tourists around the museum at Stratford upon Avon.

'This is the skull of William Shakespeare,' he told the group.

'But it's the skull of a boy!' exclaimed one tourist.

'Yes,' said the guide, blushing. 'That must have been when he was a lad.'

473. It had come to the notice of the councillors of a certain town that the man who was employed as a lavatory attendant had not had a holiday since he had been in the employ of the council. Of course, they decided that this must be seen to at once, so a time was arranged and a relief appointed. It was noticed, however, that despite the action taken on his behalf, the attendant was frequenting his place of employment, dressed in his best clothes. So one of the councillors spoke to him and asked him why he was not going away for a change as they had assumed he would. The man replied: 'Well, I am only obeying orders.'

'Obeying orders?' he queried.

'Yes,' replied the man, 'I was told that I could have a holiday at my own convenience.'

LEGAL MATTERS

474. The judge was only four feet three inches tall – a small thing sent to try us.

475. The judge found the blacksmith guilty of forging.

476. The judge had just finished telling the prisoner that he was free to go as the jury had found him not guilty of fraud, so the prisoner asked: 'Does that mean I can keep the money?'

477. A very elderly defendant had been found guilty of an offence and, as he was a habitual offender was given a stiff sentence.

'I'll never live to do it,' said the old man.

'Never mind,' said the judge in a kindly tone. 'You do what you can.'

478. The scene is a law court. The prosecution counsel faces the female witness and rasps: 'Is it true you committed adultery on the 18th of June in a snowstorm while riding on the roof of an automobile travelling at ninety miles an hour through Slough with a one-legged dwarf waving a Union Jack?'

The young woman in the witness box looked straight at the prosecuting counsel and said, calmly: 'What was the date again?'

479. A judge, in sentencing an old offender, concluded by saying: 'And I hope that this is the last time that you'll appear before me.'

'Why, Judge,' said the prisoner, 'are you retiring?'

480. The judge gave the man who stole a calendar twelve months.

481. A debtor in the dock exclaimed: 'As God is my judge, I do not owe this money.'

The judge replied: 'He's not, I am, you do.'

482. Judge: 'Have you ever been up before me before?'

Prisoner: 'I don't know, your honour. What time do you usually get up?'

483. There was an old lady named Amy who had led a blameless life but time had come for a little dare or two and she had heard how easy it was these days to do a spot of shoplifting in her spare time.

Slowly she moved along aisle after aisle of goods in the supermarket and just when she thought that she was the only one around she quickly slid a tin of tomatoes into her shopping basket. Of course, the store's cameras picked up Amy's daring deed and she found herself facing the manager and a police officer who had been called.

It didn't take long for the authorities to do their work and Amy was summoned to appear in court. The judge entered and looked down at the frail woman.

'Is this your first offence?' he wanted to know.

Amy nodded.

'Irrespective of age,' said the judge, 'we have to deal with these things harshly. Is the offending tin of tomatoes in court?' he wanted to know. The tin was produced and the clerk was instructed to open it up.

'Count how many tomatoes are in there,' the judge rasped. The clerk fumbled about with the contents and informed the court that there was exactly 6 tomatoes.

'Now listen.' The judge leaned forward as he talked to Amy. 'I am about to sentence you to 6 months. One month for each of those tomatoes that you stole.'

Amy gave a huge sigh of relief at the news. 'I will tell you something, my lord,' she said. 'I'm glad that I put that tin of baked beans back!'

484. A dry cleaner was excused jury service yesterday because he claimed his business was very pressing.

485. The father of a young lawyer thought he would try to catch his son on a legal point. Waiting until the clock struck one, he asked: 'If I were to take a hammer and smash the clock, could I be arrested for killing time?'

'Certainly not,' the son replied. 'It would be self-defence. The clock struck first.'

486. A very stout and pompous client walked into a solicitor's office, and sat on a chair which collapsed under his weight. After he had gone the solicitor remarked to his partner: 'Obnoxious fellow, that. Even the chairs can't bear him.'

487. The world-famous lawyer was holidaying on an expensive yacht when he fell overboard into a group of sharks. They declined to eat him out of professional courtesy.

488. A solicitor had a managing clerk and every morning the latter would pop out for a quick whisky, having a clove to hide the fact. One day the barman did not have any cloves but offered a pickled onion which was accepted as the next best thing.

Immediately on his return, his employer called him in for a meeting. As the clerk leaned over the table to examine a document, the solicitor suddenly asked: 'How long have you been my managing clerk?'

'About twenty years,' came the reply.

'Yes,' said the solicitor, 'and for twenty years I've put up with whisky and clove. If it's going to be whisky and pickled onion – out you go.'

489. A man stopped me in the street. He said: 'Are there any cops around?'

I said: 'You must be joking, you can never find one around here!'

He said: 'Good – stick 'em up!'

490. Policeman: 'I'm sorry, sir, but you will have to accompany me to the station.'

Simon: 'But why?'

Policeman: 'Because it's a dark and gloomy night and I'm frightened to go there on my own.'

491. A horse dropped dead in a street named Nebuchadnezzar Street and a policeman was laboriously dragging the animal round the corner into the next street.

'Whatever are you doing that for?' asked a bystander.

The policeman replied, with a knowing look: 'When I make out my report it will be easier to write "King Street" as the place of occurrence.'

492. The ace pickpocket of New York, male, married his counterpart, female, and they thought: 'If we have any children, wow! They ought to flourish in the business.'

Well, in due course a baby was born and after a while they noticed that the little one's right hand was firmly closed and despite all normal efforts to open it, it remained so. The doctor suggested a psychologist and when he saw the baby and heard what they had to say, he took the little one and, holding him gently with one arm, he took out his watch which was on a gold chain and swung it slowly before the baby's eyes. Gradually the little one's eyes followed the watch and then the little hand opened and inside was the midwife's wedding ring.

493. Joe Bloggs, a small-time jewel thief, came home after robbing a nearby country house and began to saw the legs off his bed. When his wife asked him what he was doing he replied that he wanted to 'lie low for a while'.

494. 'Is that the police?' asked a panic stricken voice on the phone to the police headquarters.

'Yes, this is the police station,' replied the officer on duty.

'Oh, thank goodness! I want to report a burglar trapped in an old lady's bedroom. Please come quickly!'

'Who is this calling?' asked the policeman.
'The burglar,' replied the voice on the phone.

495. Policeman in witness box: 'This woman came up to me when I was in plain clothes and tried to pass off this five pound note, m'lud.'
Judge: 'Counterfeit?'
Policeman in witness box: 'Yes, m'lud, she had two.'

496. A man swallowed a dud coin late last night. He is expected to be charged with passing counterfeit money later today.

497. Late last night a large hole was made in the walls surrounding Sunnyview Nudist Camp. Police are looking into it.

498. A man who beat his carpet to death a few hours ago is expected to be charged with matricide.

MARRIAGE

499. A woman threatened her husband with divorce if he continued to chase after other women. The husband begged forgiveness and solemnly swore not to pay any attention to women other than his wife.
He managed to keep his promise for a few months, but then his wife discovered him kissing a female midget.
'I'm terribly sorry,' apologised the man to his wife. 'But you must admit that I'm tapering off a bit.'

500. Jeremy: 'If you don't mind me asking, why did

your marriage to Julia break up?'

Jeffrey: 'It was due to sickness.'

Jeremy: 'I didn't know you or Julia had been ill.'

Jeffrey: 'We hadn't. I just got sick of Julia.'

501. Janice: 'My husband tricked me into marrying him. Before we married he said he was a multi-millionaire.'

Brenda: 'He *is* a multi-millionaire, isn't he?

Janice: 'Yes. But he also said he was eighty-one and in poor health – but I've just found out he's·only eighty and in perfect condition.'

502. A beautiful nineteen-year-old girl was once asked why she married a fat, balding sixty-three-year-old man who just happened to be very wealthy and own a number of large period houses.

'It's simple,' she said. 'I married him because I love his beautiful manors.'

503. One of Henry's best friends had died, so shortly after the funeral he called on the widow in order to express his sympathy.

'John and I were very good friends,' he said. 'Is there something I could have as a small memento of him?'

The widow raised her tear-stained eyes and looked at Henry. 'How would I do?' she asked, hopefully.

504. Two middle-aged men were sitting at a beach-side cafe sipping lager when one of the men said: 'Hey! Look at that fat frump in the green costume. The one jumping up and down in the sea and waving. Most hideous sight on the entire beach. Do you think all that jumping up and down and beckoning and leering towards me is some kind of proposition?'

'I don't know,' said the other man. 'If you like, I'll go down there and ask her: she's my wife!'

505. On the first morning after the honeymoon a young husband arose, went downstairs to the kitchen and took breakfast up to his bride. 'There,' he said. 'What do you think of that?'

She gazed at the tea, the bacon and eggs, the toast and marmalade, all nicely set out on the tray, and said: 'Why, that's wonderful.'

'Yes,' he replied, 'and that's how *I* want it every morning.'

506. Buried deeply in his Form book and with the television blaring the young husband absentmindedly looked over at his bouncing baby boy playing on the floor and mentioned to his wife, 'Baby's nose is running again.'

'Can't you think of anything but horses!' she snapped.

507. The married couple arrived late one night at a hotel, only to be told by the manager: 'I'm sorry, but we're full up – but you can have the bridal suite.'

'But we've been married for more than fifty years,' said the husband.

'So?' said the manager. 'I can let you have the ballroom – but you don't *have* to dance.'

508. 'Why did you marry Sarah? Was it because her father is wealthy or is she pregnant?'

'Neither. I love her.'

'Oh. I thought there would be a catch in it.'

509. Reporter: 'Why have you been married nine times?'

Hollywood actress: 'I guess it must be because I like wedding cake so much.'

510. The Hollywood film actress was getting married for the seventh time when the clergyman stumbled over the words of the ceremony.

'It's all right,' hissed the actress. 'Take it again from the top of page five.'

511. 'Hello! Is that the police station?'

'Yes.'

'Have any lunatics escaped near here recently?'

'Not that I know of, sir.'

'Oh!'

'Why do you ask?'

'Someone's run off with my wife.'

512. Clive: 'Tony, is it true you married Cynthia for the money her grandfather left her?'

Tony: 'Of course not! I would still have married her if someone else had left her the money.'

513. John: 'When I proposed to you and we got married your hair was blonde. Now it's dark brown.'

Sally: 'So? Dark brown is my natural hair colour.'

John: 'I know that, now. I was just wondering if I could sue you for bleach of promise . . .'

514. The young man asked the beautiful young girl to marry him, pointing out that his father was 103 years old and that he was heir to his father's substantial fortune.

The girl asked the young man for time to consider his offer. Two weeks later, she became his step-mother.

515. Married man: 'In your sermon this morning, vicar, you said it was wrong for people to profit from other people's mistakes. Do you really agree with that?'

Vicar: 'Of course I do.'

Married man: 'In that case, will you consider refunding the £20 I paid you for marrying me to my wife seven years ago?'

516. The happy couple proudly displayed all their wedding gifts at the reception – including an envelope from the groom's father marked 'Cheque for five hundred pounds'.

'Who is that strange man pointing at your father's cheque and laughing?' asked the bride.

The groom looked at the offending person, blinked and said: 'My father's bank manager.'

517. One day Claude came home from work to find his wife painting one side of the car blue. She'd divided the car neatly in half and had already painted the other side bright yellow.

'What on earth are you doing?' asked Claude.

'Simple!' she replied. 'You know I've had so many accidents and I always get caught due to the statements of the witnesses in court. *Now,* if I have an accident, you watch them fight it out trying to decide what colour car caused the accident!'

518. Cuthbert's wife made him a millionaire. Before he married her he was a multi-millionaire.

519. Herbert's wife was trying to take a photograph of him, so she shrieked: 'Herbert! You're not trying again. Get in focus!'

520. Henry: 'My wife made me a very unusual dinner last night: toad-in-the-hole.'

John: 'What's so unusual about that?'

Henry: 'She used real toads.'

John: 'Thank goodness she didn't try to make spotted dick . . .'

521. Sally: 'My husband gives me everything I want.'

Samantha: 'Maybe that's because you don't want enough?'

522. Ronald: 'All my wife says to me is 'Money, money'. She's always asking me for money.'

Richard: 'Why does she need so much? What does she spend it on?'

Ronald: 'I've no idea. I never give her any.'

523. Husband: 'Where is all the money I give you for household expenses going?'

Wife: 'If you will stand sideways and look in the mirror, you'll see.'

524. It was my wife's birthday. I said: 'Where do you want to go?'

She said: 'Anywhere. Take me where I've never been.'

So I took her into the kitchen.

525. Wife: 'Do you have a good memory for faces?'

Husband: 'Yes. Why?'

Wife: 'I've just broken your shaving mirror.'

526. 'Psst!' said the slimy looking man to the bridegroom. 'Do you have any photos of your wife in the nude?'

'Of course not!' growled the groom.

'Want to buy some?' asked the slimy looking man.

527. Fred: 'My wife converted me to religion.'

Bill: 'Your wife converted you to religion? How did she do that?'

Fred: 'Because I didn't believe in Hell until I married her!'

528. Senior civil servant: 'Did you phone my wife as I asked you to?'

Secretary: 'Certainly, sir. I told her you would be late home from the office due to an unexpected conference.'

Senior civil servant: 'And what did she say?'
Secretary: 'Can I rely on that?'

529. Man: 'That damn wife of mine is a liar!'
Friend: 'How do you know?'
Man: 'Because she said she spent the night with Claire.'
Friend: 'So?'
Man: '*I* spent the night with Claire!'

530. Farmer's wife: 'I'm thinking of divorcing Joe.'
Mabel: 'But why?'
Farmer's wife: 'Because he smokes in bed.'
Mabel: 'Surely that's not sufficient reason? Only smoking in bed?'
Farmer's wife: 'Ah! But Joe smokes bacon.'

531. Alan: 'I'd like to buy the woman I love a little cottage in the country where we can always be together.'
Colin: 'So why don't you?'
Alan: 'My wife won't let me.'

532. The spry old gentleman of eighty-nine had just returned from his honeymoon with his twenty-three-year-old bride.

'How did the honeymoon go?' asked a friend.

'Oh, it went quite well,' replied the old man, 'but did you ever try to get a marshmallow into a kid's piggy bank?'

533. The man was in the Army Surplus store browsing around when a shop assistant came up to him and asked: 'Can I help you, sir?'

'No, thanks,' replied the man. 'I think I've found what I want,' and he selected an army penknife. 'It's a gift for my wife,' he explained.

'Is it going to be a surprise?' asked the shop assistant.

'If so, we can gift wrap it for you.'

'Yes, please,' said the man. 'That way it will also be a double surprise – she's expecting a diamond bracelet.'

534. A sales representative combined business with pleasure and for the honeymoon took his bride with him on his travels. At one particular hotel they stayed at, he said: 'Now, they know my tastes here and there will be a pot of honey on the breakfast table.'

They came down to breakfast, sat down at the table but – no honey.

The husband called over the waitress, and said: 'Where's my honey?'

'Sorry,' said the waitress, 'she left last week.'

535. An Englishman, a Welshman and an Arab met over coffee at a convention.

'I'm happily married,' said the Englishman, 'and have 10 children. One more and I shall have my own football team.'

'I'm happily married,' said the Welshman, 'and have 14 children. One more and I shall have my own rugby team.'

'I'm also happily married,' said the Arab, 'and have 17 wives. One more and I shall have my own golf course.'

536. For the first time in twenty years, Mr and Mrs Jones decided to take their holidays apart from each other. Mrs Jones went to visit relatives in the USA, while Mr Jones went to Thailand.

The weather in Thailand was fantastic and Mr Jones had a wonderful time, especially after he met a sexy young Thai massage girl called Sunny.

Indeed, the girl and the location must have gone to his head as he sent a postcard to his wife on which he wrote: 'The weather is here. Wish you were Sunny.'

537. Man: 'My wife and I had a short row on Friday night. She wanted to go to the opera and I wanted to go to the theatre – but we soon came to an arrangement.'

Friend: 'And what was the opera like?'

538. 'Darling, I'm afraid the florist made a mistake over my anniversary order for you and they've given me these large Brazilian ferns instead of your favourite anemones.'

'That's all right, dear. They're beautiful! With fronds like these who needs anemones?'

539. Wife (at upper window) to husband who has come home late at night: 'Where have you been at this hour of the night?'

Husband: 'I've been at me union, considering this 'ere strike.'

Wife: 'Well, you can stay down there and consider this 'ere lockout.'

540. After our honeymoon I felt like a new man. My wife said she felt like one, too.

541. Jack's wife stepped on the weighing machine which also produced a fortune reading on the other side of the weight indicator card.

Out popped the card, and Jack's wife said: 'It says I'm attractive, have a pleasing personality and can charm anyone I meet.'

'Huh!' muttered Jack, taking the card from his wife. 'Even the weight is wrong!'

542. 'It was the bells that killed my husband,' sobbed the nineteen-year-old girl at the funeral of her ninety-eight-year-old husband.

'All week,' she continued, 'he would save up his strength so that we could make love on a Sunday morning. He liked to do it to the rhythm of the church

120

bells. If that stupid ice cream van hadn't gone past chiming its stupid tune I'm sure he would still be here today.'

543. A man is dragging a large box along the pavement when he suddenly stops outside one house and knocks at the door.

The door is opened by a woman, and the man asks: 'Are you Widow Jones?'

'My name is not Widow Jones,' replies the woman, 'it's Mrs Jones.'

'Wait till you see what I've got in this box,' says the man, sorrowfully.

544. 'I hear your first two wives died of mushroom poisoning. And now you tell me your third wife has just died as a result of falling off a cliff. A bit strange, isn't it?'

'Not really. She refused to eat the poisoned mushrooms.'

545. Mr Smith was just crossing a road on a zebra crossing when a car came hurtling towards him and, although he tried to jump out of the way, the car still managed to hit his side, causing him to be thrown to the ground. A loud cackling noise could be heard from the car as it sped away.

A policeman who had witnessed the accident rushed up to Mr Smith and asked: 'Did you see the driver? Or remember the car's registration number?'

'I didn't need to,' replied Mr Smith. 'It was my wife who did it.'

'How do you know?' asked the policeman.

'Simple!' replied Mr Smith. 'I'd recognise that hideous laugh anywhere.'

546. Jim is terribly sad. His wife has run off with his best friend – and he misses his friend terribly.

547. Judge: 'You've been found not guilty of bigamy, so you can now be released and go home.'

Prisoner: 'Which home shall I go to?'

548. After spending a fortune on my wife for beauty treatments I can honestly say that the only thing that makes her look good is distance.

549. I always know that if I come back from the office to a beautiful welcoming wife, with a delicious meal and fine wine on the table – I'm in the wrong house.

550. Mrs Smith: 'I've just read an interesting article. It said that most accidents that happen, happen in the kitchen.'

Mr Smith: 'I know: you always expect me to eat them.'

551. The groom turned to his best man as he finished signing the marriage register and said: 'Well, that's that! Now to go and collect a little bet.'

552. Clive: 'I can find my wife anywhere I go.'

Robert: 'How?'

Clive: 'All I have to do is open my wallet – and there she is.'

553. 'What's the trouble? You look really miserable.'

'It's Fiona, your wife.'

'My wife?'

'Yes. I'm afraid she's been unfaithful to both of us.'

554. Emma: 'But Mr Jones can't possibly be in hospital. Only last night I saw him in a restaurant looking perfectly fit and healthy with a blonde woman.'

Sally: 'So did his wife.'

555. 'Do you speak to your wife when you are making love?'

'Only if she rings up!'

556. 'I've got the most sexy, witty, creative, intelligent wife in the world . . . I just hope her husband doesn't know about it.'

557. 'Why do you call your wife Camera? Surely that's not her proper name?'

'Her real name is Gladys – but I call her Camera because she's always snapping at me.'

558. Fred: 'I call my wife a peach.'

John: 'That's nice. Is it because she's soft, sweet and juicy?'

Fred: 'No. It's because she's got a heart of stone.'

559. Joe got a letter from his wife today. It read: 'Dear Joe, I missed you yesterday. Please come home as soon as possible and let me have another shot.'

560. 'Why are you in such a hurry?'

'I'm on my way to the doctor – I don't like the look of my wife.'

'Oh! Then I'll come with you – I hate the sight of mine, too.'

561. Groom: 'Would you be very annoyed with me if I confess that all my upper teeth are false?'

Bride: 'Not at all, darling. At least I can now relax and take off my wig, inflatable bra, glass eye and artificial leg.'

562. I once knew a very sporting country gentleman who put a silencer on his shotgun because he wanted his daughter to have a quiet wedding.

563. Bill: 'I think a wife of forty should be like pound notes.'

Tom: 'In what way?'

Bill: 'You could change a wife of forty for two twenties.'

564. Claude: 'How many wives have you had?'

Fred: 'About fifteen – but only one was my own.'

565. A married man fell in love with a mermaid and everything went well with their affair until his wife began to smell something fishy . . .

566. Adrian was, as usual, complaining about his wife: 'She's always breaking her promises,' he said. 'Before we married she claimed she'd die for me – but she hasn't.'

567. 'My wife speaks through her nose.'

'Why?'

'Because she's worn out her mouth.'

568. Whenever I argue with my wife we soon patch things up – like my black eye, my broken nose, broken arm . . .

569. The seventy-nine-year-old British knight had just married a sweet, innocent seventeen-year-old debutante.

'Tell me, my dear,' said the knight. 'Did your mother explain to you the facts of life?'

'No, sir, I'm afraid she did not.'

'Oh, how awkward,' commented the knight. 'I seem to have forgotten them.'

570. Many years ago in a remote part of Ireland there lived an old Irishman and his wife. One day the old man heard that there was a fair to be held in a nearby village so he set off early in the morning to attend. Now, strange as it may seem, he had never seen a mirror before and when they were on sale at one of the stalls he bought one. When he arrived back he sat by the fire and every now and then he took out the mirror from his pocket and glanced at it, hurriedly putting it back when his wife asked him what he was looking at. 'Never you mind, woman,' he said.

Well, she was curious, so after her husband was in bed and asleep, she searched his clothes and found the mirror. She looked at it long and earnestly, then said: 'As I thought, another woman.'

571. An aeroplane found itself in trouble and crashed in the jungle, leaving only one survivor, a beautiful, long limbed blonde who would have been the envy of many female film stars. She was thrown from the plane before it exploded, only to land at the feet of a cannibal and his son. The son circled his quarry, licking his lips at such a feast dropping from the sky.

'Can I have the first bite of her?' he asked his dad.

The adult cannibal also circled the beautiful form before him but his mind wasn't on the dinner table.

'I'll tell you what,' he touched the lad with his spear. 'Let's take *her* home . . . and eat your Mum!'

572. Another clever cannibal toasted his mother-in-law at the wedding dinner.

573. The couple had just reached retirement age, but Mr Robinson was a very worried man.

'We don't really have enough to live on,' he confessed to his wife. 'Sure, our pension is enough to survive – but we lack sufficient savings to give us a few extra pleasures like the occasional evening at the cinema or a decent holiday once a year.'

'Don't worry,' replied Mrs Robinson. 'I've managed to save a few thousand pounds.'

'However did you manage that?'

'Well,' said Mrs Robinson, a bit shyly, 'every time you made love to me these past thirty years I've put fifty pence in my own bank account.'

'But why did you keep it a secret all these years?' demanded Mr Robinson. 'If I'd known about it I'd have given you all my business.'

574. Mr Smith's wife decided to make an unexpected visit to her husband's office in order to take a look at his new secretary.

'You liar!' hissed Mrs Smith to her husband. 'You told me that your new secretary was very efficient and capable but that she looked like a horrible old hag. But I've just seen her and she's about eighteen years old, extremely pretty and . . .'

'But she's *not* my secretary,' interrupted Mr Smith, who had been thinking very rapidly. 'My secretary is ill today and so she sent her grand-daughter to help out instead.'

575. A husband went off to see a rugby match and he hadn't been gone very long when an old flame of his wife called. This chap was on a hike and wearing shorts and a jersey, and as it had started to pour with rain, being in the district he had looked her up. They were talking about old times when suddenly a key was heard turning in the lock – the husband had returned. Quick as a flash the woman said: 'You'd better hide, for you remember he never liked you.' So the chap ducked down behind the rather large television set that was in the room.

When the husband entered he said: 'It has come on to rain very hard, not at all nice, and as I find that the second half is being televised, I've come back to see it in comfort.'

After a time the chap behind the television set was getting cramp, so he decided to make a bold gesture, and he rose up and walked out of the room without saying a word. Then the husband turned to his wife and said: 'Funny, I never saw the ref send him off.'

576. She could tell from the moment that he entered the bedroom that her husband was in a mocking mood. As she stood peacefully combing her hair, looking into the wardrobe mirror, she caught a glimpse of him stealing stealthily towards her. He played his hands along her back then quietly moved them to her chest.

'If those were more firm you wouldn't have to rely on a bra so often,' he said. She gave a shrug and let the remark pass.

Slowly his hands touched her bottom. 'If that was more firm you wouldn't have to rely on a girdle so often,' he sneered.

By this time his wife had had enough, and swinging round she caught him square in the groin which brought tears to his eyes. 'And if *that* had been more firm,' she snapped, 'I wouldn't have had to rely on your brother so often!'

577. You can always find my husband at a party, even if you've never met him before. All you have to do is find a situation where two people are talking – if one of them looks extremely bored, then it's my husband who's doing the talking.

578. My husband keeps boasting to people at parties that he has more than a thousand people under him. So he does – he's a gardener in a cemetery.

579. A widow had a gravestone erected and in large letters RIP was inscribed after the wording.

Later she found out that, unknown to her, her late husband had been a womaniser and had had several romantic episodes in the village. To satisfy herself she went around to the stonemason and asked if he would add three more words to the gravestone. When he asked what were the words, she said: 'Please add, "until *I* come".'

580. Whilst passing a cemetery one afternoon I heard a sad, heart-rending voice sobbing and repeating: 'Why did you have to go?'

Naturally, I couldn't just carry on and go home leaving the scene as it was, so I turned around, entered the cemetery and walked in the direction from where the voice was coming.

Sure enough, bent on his knees over a grave was a weedy looking man with tears in his eyes, still repeating: 'Why did you have to go?'

'Was it your wife?' I asked, in my best bedside manner.

The man looked up with tears running from his eyes. 'Eh?' he said.

'Was it your wife?' I asked again.

'No,' he answered. 'It was the wife's first husband!'

581. A hillbilly boy from Nashville, Tennessee, announces to his folks: 'I's a'goin to Knoxville, to fetch me a wife.'

A few days later he returns with a nubile young sweetheart called Mary Lou. She is introduced to all the family, cramped around the kitchen table of their tiny shack.

Come six o'clock his father says: 'Well, my boy, I guess you two deserve the family bedroom now. Your Maw and Paw can sleep down here.' So the happy couple go off upstairs. Half an hour later a shotgun blast rattles the timbers, and then the son clambers slowly down the steps from above.

'Whatever happened?' inquired his mother.

'I shot her,' said the son.

'Why?'

'She was a virgin.'

The boy's Grandpa, who had sat quietly through all these proceedings, was the first to break the thunder-struck silence: 'Son, I guess you did the right thing – if she was no good to nobody in *her* family, then she ain't no use to any of us!'

582. Some British Army officers were on leave and one, a young lieutenant, entered a hairdressers' for a trim. He hadn't been seated many minutes when a colonel – but not in the same regiment – entered and sat next to him. Presently the hairdresser asked the lieutenant: 'Would you like some dressing on your hair, sir?'

'Good heavens, no,' he replied. 'I don't want my wife to think I've just come out from some brothel!'

Then it was the turn of the colonel to be asked the same question to which he replied loudly, for the benefit of the lieutenant who had not yet left the establishment: 'Rather! Put as much as you like on. *My* wife doesn't know what a brothel smells like!'

583. 'Where did you get such a nice suit?'

'It was a present from my wife. I came home unexpectedly early from the office the other evening, and there it was – hanging over the back of a chair in the bedroom.'

584. Janet: 'My husband is no good.'

Julia: 'But I thought you told me last week that he was a model husband?'

Janet: 'He is a model husband – but not a working model.'

585. My wife has asthma and finds it difficult to breathe on occasions. Yesterday she got a dirty phone call.

After 40 seconds the voice on the phone said: 'Did I call you or did you call me?'

586. 'I didn't make love to my wife before we were married. Didn't believe in that sort of thing. Did you?'

'Don't know. What did you say your wife's name was?'

587. My husband is so stupid he thinks a crap game is where people take bets on who can throw dried cow droppings the farthest.

588. Tom: 'There's one word that describes my wife: temperamental.'

John: 'In what way?'

Tom: 'She's fifty per cent temper and fifty per cent mental!'

589. 'What did you do before you got married to Gloria?'

'Anything I wanted to do.'

590. The solicitor was reading Humphrey's will and had just come to the last paragraph. 'I always said I'd mention my dear wife, Joan, in my will,' read out the solicitor. 'So, hello there, Joan.'

591. John: 'My wife's a kelptomaniac.'

Richard: 'Is she taking anything for it?'

592. Millicent: 'My husband's career is in ruins.'

Mary: 'Oh, I'm sorry to hear that.'

Millicent: 'There's nothing to be sorry about. He's an archaeologist.'

593. Many a wife has helped her husband to the top of the ladder and then left him there while she considered whether the picture would look better somewhere else.

594. Susan has been married and divorced so many times to wealthy men she is getting richer by decrees.

595. Eve was so jealous of Adam that when he came home each night she used to count his ribs.

596. David was out all night with the glamorous hostess from a notorious Soho nightclub. When he returned home at five o'clock in the morning he tried to sneak into bed with his wife without waking her. But he was unsuccessful and she turned on the bedside light and watched her husband undress before putting on his pyjamas.

'Where is your underwear?' she demanded, when it was obvious that David had not been wearing any before he had started to undress.

'My God!' cried David in anguish. 'I've been robbed!'

597. It's dangerous to talk in your sleep, as my neighbour found out. When in bed with his wife he was having a restless night and as he tossed and turned he kept repeating 'Eva, darling', when his wife's name was Joan.

When he came downstairs in the morning he expected breakfast on the table as usual but the table was bare. After asking what was going on he was told by his wife of his murmurings overnight. She insisted on knowing who Eva was.

'You kept on saying "Eva, darling", over and over again.'

He knew that he had to think of something quick. 'Eva Darling is the name of a runner at Ascot,' he said, and she accepted it.

Thinking that all was well he happily breezed through the day's work, but on getting home he found that the expected tea wasn't forthcoming.

'Not again!' he moaned. 'And what is the reason this time?'

'Your race horse rang this afternoon,' he was told.

598. It was a dull day and Alf had come home from work feeling as depressed as the weather. Things hadn't been right at work for a long time and Alf had let his depression follow him home.

Alf's wife had gone out of her way to please her husband with a meal she had prepared as instructed at evening classes, but all Alf did was to sniff at his plate before pushing it back along the table. His wife knew that there was something not quite right with their marriage, so she decided to find out just what it was.

'You aren't the same woman that I married,' protested Alf. 'You leave the eyes in the potatoes, my shirt has creases where they shouldn't be, you don't remake the bed every day . . . and whilst I'm on that subject, you don't moan when we make love!'

'But I could do . . .' answered the meek woman.

That night in bed, Alf went into his amorous escapades and his wife was eager to please.

'Shall I moan now?' asked the lady.

'Not yet,' answered Alf, who wanted things to be just so. Another few minutes went by.

'Shall I moan now?' came the female voice.

Knowing that things were about to come to an end, Alf gave permission for moaning to begin. 'Go on . . . moan.'

There was silence for a few seconds, then the female voice began to moan: 'What about those shelves you promised to put up?' she moaned. 'This bedroom wants decorating . . . you can stop going to the pub at Sunday lunchtime, the garden wants . . .'

599. It was in olden days and the bride and groom were setting off alone on their honeymoon – travelling by horse and carriage.

Suddenly, the horse reared up, startled by a snake in its path. Annoyed at the horse's behaviour, the man waved his finger threateningly at the horse and said: 'That's your first warning.'

They continued their journey until about half an hour later when the horse stopped at a water trough at the roadside to drink a few sips of water.

Again, the man was annoyed at this interruption in their journey, and he wagged his finger and said, menacingly: 'That's the second warning.'

They continued their journey until dusk, when again the horse reared up, rocking the carriage violently. The man clambered down from the carriage, took out his gun, and shot the horse dead between the eyes, saying as he did this: 'And that was the third time.'

The man's wife, on seeing this, burst into tears. 'What did you shoot the horse for? She was probably frightened by another snake or something similar. It wasn't her fault. Now you've killed her! How could you be so cruel! If I'd known you were such a sadist I'd never have married you! How could you do it to such a poor defenceless creature?'

As she began to cry uncontrollably, her husband wagged his finger at her and said: 'That's the first warning.'

600. A girl was going to be married, but as the wedding day approached she grew nervous. This was noticed by her mother who asked if there was anything the matter.

'Not really,' replied the girl, 'but it's the thought of going away on honeymoon that's troubling me.'

'Now, my dear,' said her mother, 'don't let that worry you. Why, I went off on my honeymoon.'

'Ah! It was all right for you,' retorted the daughter, 'you went away with Dad!'

601. The woman wearing an enormous flowery hat was stopped at the entrance to the church by one of the ushers.

'Are you a friend of the bride?' asked the usher.

'Of course not!' snapped the woman. 'I'm the groom's mother.'

602. Mr and Mrs Smith, a childless couple, had been married fifty years. They had always had many friends and so did not fret about never having any children.

The Golden Wedding Anniversary celebrations had been very successful and so it was a slightly drunk Mr and Mrs Smith who went to bed shortly after the last guest had left.

In bed, Mrs Smith lay and looked at the ceiling as she said: 'You know, all this festivity brings back memories of our wedding.'

'And our honeymoon,' said Mr Smith.

'Yes. It was a pity we were both so young and inexperienced then. Sixteen really was too young for people in those days to have got married. Of course, young people today know far more about the facts of life than we ever did when we first got married.'

'I know, dear,' replied Mr Smith. 'Young people today wouldn't have had the same difficulties we had on our wedding night.'

'Darling,' said Mrs Smith, 'would you like to try again?'

603. 'We've had six happy, glorious years. Mind you, we've been married for twenty-five!'

604. Every woman worries about the future until she has acquired a husband, whereas men never worry about the future until they get a wife.

605. I wouldn't say my husband was stupid – but when he went to a mind reader they gave him his money back.

606. My husband insists he's not bald – just that his hair is flesh coloured.

607. The only thing my husband ever achieved on his own is his moustache.

608. The reason my husband is so thin is because when he went to donate blood he forgot to say 'when'.

609. My husband only tells jokes after he's drunk a whole bottle of whisky. It seems he has a rye sense of humour.

610. My husband never gets a hangover – he's always drunk.

611. If my husband ever had any get-up-and-go it got up and went before I met him.

612. My husband isn't exactly stupid – it's just that he's been educated beyond his intelligence.

613. My husband is a self-made man who loves his maker.

614. My husband is so short-sighted he can't go to sleep unless he counts elephants.

615. My husband is such a hypochondriac he refused to kiss me until I bought lipstick with penicillin in it.

616. My husband believes so devoutly in reincarnation his Will leaves everything to himself.

617. My husband's clothes will never go out of style – they'll always look ridiculous.

618. My husband is so thin that whenever he goes to the park the ducks throw *him* bread.

619. My husband always drinks with a friend – that way he's got someone to carry him home.

620. My husband has given me something to live for – revenge!

621. There's nothing wrong with my wife that a good funeral wouldn't cure.

622. My wife has a slight impediment in her speech. Every now and then she has to stop to take a breath.

623. The best years of my wife's life were the twenty between eighteen and twenty-nine.

624. A month ago my wife put mud all over her face to improve her looks. It improved them so much she hasn't taken the mud off yet.

625. My wife and I never argue. She always goes her way and I always go hers.

626. My wife has had her face lifted so many times that now they have to lower her body.

627. My wife is so fat – if she was a stripper she'd have to wear a G-rope.

628. My wife has a better sense of judgment than I have – she chose me as her husband.

629. My wife treats me like a pagan god. Every evening at dinner time she gives me a burnt offering.

630. I wouldn't say my wife pushed much dirt under the carpet – but I have to walk uphill to the fireplace.

631. My wife says I'm effeminate. Compared to her, I suppose I am.

632. One man I know hasn't spoken to his wife for ten years – he's far too polite to interrupt her talking.

633. My wife insists she's not fat – just that she's three feet too short for her body.

634. My wife takes three hours to eat a plate of alphabet soup – she insists on eating it alphabetically.

635. My wife had plastic surgery last week – I cut off her credit card.

636. My wife's left me. I think she's gone for good this time. She's taken her bingo pens.

MONEY

637. Brian: 'You must think I'm absolutely stupid, asking me to invest in such a crackpot scheme.'

Fred: 'So can I put you down for a few thousand, then . . . ?'

638. Within a few weeks of winning a fortune on the national lottery an elderly tramp died of a heart attack. In his will he decreed that most of his money was to be used for upholstering as many park benches as possible.

639. Grandma was nearly ninety years of age when she won £1,000,000 on the premium bonds. Her family were extremely worried about her heart and feared that the news of her large win would come as too much of a shock for her.

'I think we had better call in the doctor to tell her the

news,' suggested the eldest son.

The doctor soon arrived and the situation was explained to him.

'Now, you don't have to worry about anything,' said the doctor. 'I am fully trained in such delicate matters and I feel sure I can break this news to her gently. I assure you, there is absolutely no need for you to fear for her health. Everything will be quite safe if left to me.'

The doctor went in to see the old lady and gradually brought the conversation around to premium bonds.

'Tell me,' said the doctor, 'what would you do if you had a large win on the bonds – say one million pounds?'

'Why,' replied the old lady, 'I'd give half of it to you, of course.'

The doctor fell down dead with shock.

640. When Edward called on his friend, Arnold (who was something of a miser), he found Arnold carefully stripping the wallpaper.

'Are you re-decorating?' asked Edward.

'Of course not!' replied Arnold. 'I'm moving.'

641. The easiest way to return from Las Vegas with a small fortune is to go there with a very large fortune.

642. Robber, brandishing a gun: 'Your money or your life.'

Mr Smith: 'You'd better take my life. I'm saving my money for my old age.'

643. John: 'I've got a terrible problem. I've got a flat in Mayfair, an apartment in Spain, a condominium in Acapulco and I've just bought a three thousand acre estate in Surrey and my third Rolls Royce.'

Simon: 'What's wrong with that? You appear to be doing very well.'

John: 'But I only earn two hundred pounds a week!'

644. The party of American hog slaughterers had been touring London for several days, visiting all the sights and being accompanied by various tour guides.

'Tell me,' said one of the Americans to a tour guide, 'what's this "aristocracy" that you keep talking about? Who or what are they?'

'"Aristocracy",' replied the guide, 'is a collective noun used to describe a group of people who owe their position to their parents who, in turn, owe it to theirs and so on. The position is such that they need not do much and generally lead a life of leisure without having to bother much about earning money by hard work.'

'Oh!' said the American who had asked the question. 'We have people like that in the USA too, only we call them tramps or hoboes.'

645. Twenty years ago I used to dream about the time when I would be living in fantastic luxury on the same wages that are now keeping me below the poverty line.

646. A man went to see his bank manager to ask for a loan. After he had taken particulars, the bank manager said: 'By rights I should refuse your request, but I will give you a sporting chance. Now, one of my eyes is made of glass. If you can tell me which one it is, I will grant you the loan.'

The customer looked at the other intently for a few moments and then said: 'It's your right eye.'

'That's correct,' said the bank manager. 'How did you guess?'

'Well,' replied the customer, 'it appeared to be more sympathetic.'

647. Customer: 'And how do I stand for a £20,000 loan?'

Bank Manager: 'You don't – you grovel.'

648. Mr Williams was angry with his son, who just

seemed to laze about the house all day, even though he had been given a good education and was now 22 years old.

'You can't hang around waiting for a top job to come along,' said Mr Williams. 'You've got to start somewhere. Why don't you do the same as I did? Start as a humble accounts clerk. Within five years I'd made enough to start my own business.'

'I know, Dad,' replied the son, 'but that's not possible these days – they have proper auditors now!'

649. It is easy for a beggar to tell the difference between a politician and an accountant. If he asks a man for money for a meal saying he hasn't eaten all day, and the man replies: 'Sorry, no. But things will be better for you tomorrow' – that man must be a politician.

If the beggar asks the same question and a man replies: 'Sorry, no. But I'm interested to know how your financial situation compares with the same period last month ' – then that man must be an accountant.

650. The income tax authorities have now produced a new, simple tax form with only two sections:

(a) How much do you earn?
(b) Send it.

651. One of the turns at a variety entertainment was a strong man who took a lemon in his hand and squeezed it so hard that apparently not a further drop of juice remained. He then offered £20 to any member of the audience who could manage to squeeze a few more drops. At first no one volunteered, then a little, middle-aged man rose to his feet and said that he would like to try.

Taking the lemon firmly in his hand he pressed very hard until a thin trickle ran out. The strong man was astonished and asked the other if he, too, was a performer.

'No,' replied the little man, 'I'm an Income Tax Collector.'

652. The tax inspector received an income tax return from a bachelor executive claiming a dependent son. He thought this was rather odd, so he sent back the form with a note stating: 'This must be a typist's error.'

Back came the form from the exccutive, together with a pencilled marginal comment next to the inspcctor's saying: 'You're telling me.'

OFFICES & SALESMEN

653. A businessman had three trays on his desk marked: 'In', 'Out' and 'LBW'.

A client asked him what was the meaning of LBW, and the businessman explained: 'Oh, that means "Let the blighters wait"!'

654. The television company decided to make a programme about successful business executives, so they called five of them into the studio to talk about their lives and how they managed to be so successful.

The first four executives all told of how they had fought to get to the top – all four of them marrying their respective boss's daughter. But the fifth executive had had a really hard fight to become successful.

'Life was never easy for me,' he explained. 'I had to fight for everything and times were often extremely difficult – but I just gritted my teeth, rolled up my sleeves . . . and got down to asking Dad to lend me another £500,000.'

655. Angry employer: 'You should have been here at nine o'clock.'

Late employee: 'Why, what happened?'

656. 'Have you had a busy day at the office?' a young woman asked her husband when he arrived home a little late.

'Terrible,' he replied. 'The computer broke down in the middle of the afternoon and we all had to think.'

657. Office manager: 'Clara, you've been seen kissing a number of the male clerks in the stationery cupboard; have been observed cuddling the messenger boy; and today I find you canoodling with a trainee accountant. What sort of a reference can I possibly give you after that sort of behaviour?'

Trainee secretary: 'Perhaps you could say that while I was training I tried my best to please as many people as possible in the office.'

658. Angry employer, berating his sweet young secretary: 'Who told you that you could have the morning off just to go shopping? And now you have the cheek to ask for a salary increase – merely because you came with me as my assistant to the conference in Brussels last weekend! Who gives you encouragement for such fantastic ideas?'

Secretary: 'My legal adviser, sir.'

659. Filing cabinet: a useful container where things can be lost alphabetically.

660. A businessman was asked by a friend: 'Why does your new secretary wear such a long bead necklace?'

He replied: 'She wants me to know that I can count on her.'

142

661. Boss: 'Did you take any messages while I was out?'

Young secretary: 'No. Are any of them missing?'

662. Personnel Manager: 'How well can you type?'

Young secretary: 'My typing isn't very good – but I can erase at sixty-five words per minute!'

663. Personnel Manager: 'Can you do shorthand?'

Young secretary: 'Yes, but it takes me longer.'

664. The boss leaned over his secretary, who was busily painting her fingernails, and said: 'Miss Ruggles, I'd like to compliment you on your work – but when are you going to do any?'

665. New secretary: 'You seem to know your way around very well. How long have you been working here?'

Secretary: 'Ever since the boss told me he'd sack me if I didn't.'

666. Fred: 'My secretary is a biblical secretary.'

John: 'A biblical secretary? What's that?'

Fred: 'One who believes in filing things according to the Bible saying: "Seek and ye shall find".'

667. Angry employer: 'Why are you late again this morning?'

Young typist: 'I overslept.'

Angry employer: 'You mean, you sleep at home *as well*?'

668. One boss had to fire eleven secretaries because of the mistakes they wouldn't make.

669. My secretary is called 'Good Time' – because she's the good time that's been had by all.

670. At the Company Board meeting the Chairman rose to make his speech. 'Who has been carrying on with my secretary?' he demanded.

This was met with silence. 'All right, then,' said the Chairman, 'put it this way – who has *not* been carrying on with my secretary?'

Again there was silence, and then one man said, self-consciously: 'Me, sir.'

'Right,' said the Chairman. '*You* sack her.'

671. His secretary thinks she's clever. She's joined as many unions as possible so she gets more chances of being called out on strike.

672. Office manager: 'Look at all the dust on this desk! It looks as if it hasn't been cleaned for a fortnight.'

Cleaner: 'Don't blame me, sir. I've only been here a week.'

673. The last time I sat on a committee we were presented with a plan which had two alternatives. We therefore narrowed it down to eighteen possibilities for further discussion.

674. The difference between a good committee member and a bad committee member is that a good one sleeps upright and a bad one sleeps horizontally.

675. A commercial traveller, snowbound in the Orkneys, wired his firm in Aberdeen: 'Marooned here by snowstorm. Send instructions.'

The reply came back: 'Start summer holidays as from yesterday.'

676. At an international sales exhibition, one British salesman turned to another and asked: 'How are you faring so far today?'

'Quite well,' replied the other salesman. 'I've picked

up lots of useful information, followed up a number of promising leads, renewed relationships with a number of potential customers and made a lot of valuable new contacts.'

'So have I,' responded the first salesman. 'I haven't sold anything yet, either.'

677. The manager of a firm wanted his salesman to spend a couple of months away on a special job, but the salesman was recently married and explained the strain of the thought of what he would be missing at home.

'Get what you want in that line and charge it to the firm,' the boss suggested.

'But when I send in my expense form what will your secretary think about it?'

'There's no need to put down exactly what it's for,' said the boss. 'Just put "knocking nails in wood". I'll know what it's for.'

The salesman duly obliged and weekly expense sheets came in with an item: 'knocking nails in wood – £200' and nothing was thought of it.

One day an expense sheet came in from the salesman which the secretary took straight to the boss, querying the charge.

'Look here,' she said to the boss. 'On this expense sheet for our salesman there's an item "knocking nails in wood – £200".'

'Well,' said the boss. 'I've told you to pay it.'

'That's OK,' said the secretary, 'but look at this: "Repairs to hammer shaft – £1,000".'

678. The little old lady was busy dusting with her feather duster in her little old cottage deep in the countryside when there was a knock on the door.

'Good morning, madam,' said a suave young man when she opened the door, and he pushed his way into the house, saying: 'What a lovely house, but I'm sure you'll be interested in what I can offer you.'

'But . . .' started the old woman, before being interrupted by the young man who had by now pulled a large bag of soot, dust and other small items of rubbish from his pocket and was sprinkling them all over the carpet.

'Don't worry,' said the young man. 'What I have in my car outside will soon remove all this rubbish, dust and soot and I'll even demonstrate by cleaning your other rooms, too. So effective is my new machine that it will even suck out ground-in dust and dirt like this,' and he used his heel to drive into the pile of the carpet some of the soot.

'But . . .' tried the old lady again, but to no avail as the young man had rapidly gone out of the front door and soon reappeared with a vacuum cleaner.

'Now, where can I plug this in?' he asked.

'Probably the next village, about ten miles away,' replied the old lady. 'The electricity supply hasn't reached here yet!'

679. I've just bought a retirement policy. If I keep paying the premiums for thirty-five years the insurance salesman can retire rich.

PEOPLE

680. I once went to a jumble sale and bought a very old and very large bureau. While I was cleaning it I must have pressed a secret button and a large panel in the back of the bureau popped open and three people fell out, shouting: 'Where am I? Where am I?' That's how I realized I must have bought a missing persons bureau.

681. Sally: 'Whenever I see a mirror I can never resist looking into it for at least a few minutes to admire my flawless complexion. Do you think that's vanity?'

Samantha: 'No. More like imagination.'

682. 'I've got an amazing watch. It only cost me 50p.'

'Why is it so amazing?'

'Because every time I look at it I'm amazed it's still working.'

683. There was a knock on the door. Mr Jones sighed and said to his wife: 'I bet it's that Bloggis fellow from next door wanting to borrow something else. He's already borrowed half the things in our house!'

'I know, dear,' replied Mrs Jones. 'But why do you have to give in to him every time? Why not make some excuse so he can't borrow whatever he's come to borrow?'

'Good idea!' agreed Mr Jones and he went and opened the door to Bloggis.

'Good morning,' said Bloggis. 'I'm sorry to trouble you, but I wondered if you would be using your garden shears this afternoon?'

'I'm afraid I will,' responded Mr Jones. 'In fact, my wife and I will be spending the whole afternoon gardening.'

'That's what I thought,' said Mr Bloggis. 'Now I know you'll be too busy to use your golf clubs, so perhaps you won't mind if I borrow them?'

684. An old boy had fallen down in the road and some people came to his aid and helped him to his feet. As he started to move he staggered and an old lady asked: 'Oh, my good man. Have you vertigo?'

'No, mam,' replied the old boy. 'Only just around the corner.'

685. Sammy was walking down the street with two

bricks under his arm.

'What are you doing with those bricks?' his friend asked.

'I'm going to Harry's house. He put a brick through my window last night.'

'But why the two bricks?' he was asked.

'Well, you see, he's got double glazing.'

686. As a wedding anniversary gift, Frank Smith bought his wife an answerphone. The first day she got it she fitted it up to say: 'This is the Smith residence. Unfortunately, Mrs Smith is out but you can leave a message. Please start your rumour or gossip after the tone . . .'

687. Alan was boring everyone at the party. 'Yes,' he said, 'I've hunted all over India and Africa.'

'Oh?' asked a little old lady. 'What did you lose?'

688. A landlord wrote to one of his tenants, asking him if he wished to renew the lease of the premises he was occupying. He received this brief answer: 'Dear Sir, I remain, Yours faithfully.'

689. The Americans quickly proved that the Moon was uninhabited as one of the first things they did when they landed was to dig a hole. Since no one came to stand around and watch they knew that no one lived there.

690. An old woman had the reputation for always saying something good about folk and never saying anything unkind about them.

One day a neighbour remarked: 'Why, I do believe that you'd say a good word about the devil himself!'

To which she replied: 'Well, he may not be as good as he ought to be, but he's a real industrious body, for all that.'

691. A young girl visits a clairvoyant, who, looking into her crystal ball, bursts out laughing. With a crack like a pistol shot, the girl slaps the medium hard across the jaw.

'*Ouch*! What was *that* for?' protests the fortune teller.

'My mother always insists that I should strike a happy medium!' the child explains.

692. The grand old man at the Home was celebrating his 112th birthday and the reporter from the local newspaper asked him: 'Tell me, what do you think is the reason for your long life?'

The old man thought for a moment, then said: 'Well, I suppose it's because I was born such a long time ago.'

693. John: 'I just don't know what to do. What would *you* do if you were in my shoes?'

Alan: 'Polish them.'

694. Janice: 'I'm feeling rather homesick.'

George: 'But you *are* at home.'

Janice: 'I know. But I'm sick of it.'

695. 'Would you like to come to my house-warming party on Friday?'

'I'd love to! What's the address?'

'Number six, Labrador Crescent. Just ring the bell with your elbow.'

'Why can't I ring it with my finger?'

'You're not coming empty-handed, are you?'

696. A little girl's thank you note: 'Thank you for your nice present. I always wanted a pin cushion, but not very much.'

697. Four women were sitting talking and discussing their faults. Said one: 'I must confess that I'm fond of a gamble and I bet quite a bit. Once I lost the whole of my week's housekeeping money.'

'Well,' said another, 'I don't gamble, but I do like a drink and I'm afraid that when my husband is away and I am alone, I sometimes get quite tiddly.'

'My great trouble,' said the third woman, 'is that I can't help flirting. I just like having a slight affair now and then. Once, however, it nearly landed me in serious trouble.'

They all turned to the fourth woman and asked: 'Have you any faults?'

'Yes,' she replied. 'My only real fault is that I am a great gossip.'

698. Nelson was dying on board HMS *Victory*. He looked up, sadly, and said: 'Kiss me, Hardy!'

Hardy looked down and muttered: 'All these years on the same ship and *now* he asks me!'

699. Tim: 'What's your New Year's Resolution?'

Frank: 'To be much less conceited.'

Tim: 'Will that be difficult to maintain for a year?'

Frank: 'Not for someone as clever and intelligent as me.'

700. 'I bet you don't know how many sheep there are in this field?' said the English farmer to the Irish visitor.

The Irishman glanced around the field and then replied: 'Three hundred and eighty-six.'

The farmer was astonished. 'That's incredible! You're perfectly right. How did you manage it?'

'Oh, it was quite simple,' said the Irishman. 'I just counted the number of legs and divided by four.'

701. Henrietta (talking on the phone): 'Can I speak to someone in the mail order department?'

Voice on the phone: 'Speaking.'

Henrietta: 'Oh. I'd like to order one. About thirty to thirty-five, fairly tall, reasonably well-off, and who likes animals.'

702. A dignified clergyman who was very fond of children, set out one night to attend a party given 'by children for children'.

'Don't announce me,' he said to the master of ceremonies, on arrival.

Leaving his coat and hat downstairs, he quietly opened the door of the drawing room, where the buzz of voices announced the presence of company. Dropping on his hands and knees, he entered making funny noises distinctly resembling the braying of a donkey. Aware of a dead silence, he looked up and found the guests regarding him with alarm. The children's party was next door.

703. An old lady, a spinster, visited an undertaker as she felt that she would like to make her own funeral arrangements in advance so that when the time came there would be no trouble in carrying out her wishes.

The undertaker was very kind and said that it was usual to line the coffin for a single lady in white – that for a married woman was mauve. The old lady said she quite understood but just as she was leaving she whispered to him: 'I think I'd better have just a little bit of mauve.'

704. A country yokel and a professor were in a train, and as it was a long journey they eventually got to talking.

'Every time you miss a riddle you give me a pound, and every time I miss one I give you a pound,' said the professor, when they had run out of the usual things to talk about.

'Ah, but you're better educated than me, so I'll give

you 50p and you give me a quid,' suggested the yokel.

The professor agreed and the yokel made up the first riddle: 'What has three legs walking and two legs flying?'

The professor didn't know, so he gave the yokel a pound. The yokel didn't know either, so he gave the professor 50p.

705. An Englishman, an Irishman, a Scotsman and an American, hitherto complete strangers to each other, were shipwrecked on a desert island. The natives were friendly and in a short time the American was running a light railway, the Scot was running a store, the Irishman was training an army, while the Englishman was waiting to be introduced.

706. There is a story told that it used to be the practice of the Salvation Army to play outside the former Charing Cross Hospital every Sunday afternoon. On one occasion the matron, on going to a ward which faced the street, saw a number of soldier patients throwing money out of the window to the band below.

She congratulated them on their generosity and then wondered why they all looked so sheepish after she had spoken. Then one of the men said: 'Look here, Matron, you thought we were giving money to the Salvation Army. We weren't really. We had made a bet as to the one who could throw a penny down the big trumpet first.'

707. A lady was having an argument with her maid. Before leaving the room the maid decided to say exactly what she thought.

'You might like to know,' she said, 'that your husband told me only last week that I am a far better housekeeper and cook than you are. He also said I was much better looking!'

The lady remained silent.

'And that's not all,' continued the maid. 'I'm far better than you in bed.'

'I suppose my husband told you that as well!' snapped the lady.

'No,' replied the maid, 'the gardener did.'

708. John was always boasting. In fact, he was probably the biggest boaster in the world – and the most conceited. He was also incredibly fat and must have weighed at least twenty-five stone.

People were therefore surprised when John died and his coffin appeared to be extremely small.

'Is that really John in there?' asked one of the people at the funeral.

'Of course!' was the reply. 'When all the wind was let out of him he only needed a small coffin.'

709. I was watching a funeral the other day and upon the coffin lay a fishing rod, a reel and a fishing basket. I said to a fellow next to me: 'He must have been a very keen fisherman?'

The man turned to me and said: 'He still is. He's going straight to a fishing match after they've buried his wife.'

710. A shipwrecked sailor had been drifting about on a raft for weeks, when one day he suddenly sighted land. As he came closer to the shore he saw a group of people on the beach building a gallows.

'Thank God!' cried the shipwrecked sailor. 'A Christian country!'

711. Albert walked into the club. 'Your eye is black!' said his mate.

'Yes, it's seenus.'

'Don't you mean sinus?'

'No. Her husband's seen us!'

Within the hour another man walked in with a black eye.

'Who's given you that?'

'They don't give you these. You have to fight for them.'

712. It was ten years since William and Derek had left school and in those ten years they had not met. Then, at the school reunion dinner, they sat next to each other.

'How has life treated you since leaving school?' asked Derek.

'Oh, I've had my ups and downs. But now I'm doing quite well as an estate agent. We've got offices in fifteen towns and villages in the area and hope to open a London branch next year.'

'That sounds good,' replied Derek.

'And how have you done since leaving school?' asked William.

'Not so good,' said Derek. 'You know when I was at school I fancied Fiona? Well, I married her soon after school – but within three months of marriage she left me for another man. Then my second wife ran off with her girlfriend. The new house I bought by the sea was a bit too near it – within a year after buying it the cliff it was on fell into the sea, taking the house and all my possessions with it. And you probably saw that I walk with a limp. That's the result of falling out of my canoe and being crushed against a weir. And today didn't start too well, either. My dog was run over and killed by a bus and my motorcycle was set on fire by vandals.'

'But, if you don't mind me asking,' said William, 'what do you do for a living?'

'Oh!' replied Derek, 'I sell good luck charms.'

713. Three dishevelled, bearded men sat forlornly upon their upturned empty beer barrels as the sea waves lapped at their feet on the edge of their desert island. Having been imprisoned there for the last three years the first man stretched his arms to the sun and yawned, just to break the monotony. The second pretended that he had a comb and began to comb whilst the third looked down with a smile upon his face.

Toying away with his big toe was a bottle bobbing about in the water. The man picked it up and seeing that it was empty was about to throw it back into the sea when he decided to take out the cork.

Immediately a puff of smoke appeared from the neck and grew larger with every second until it resembled a man of Arabian descent.

'I am the Genie of the bottle,' it told them. 'I have been enslaved in here for a thousand years.'

'It seems that we've been enslaved here for that long too,' the first man told the visitor.

'For your good deed you can each have a wish. So think it over carefully because it will be the only one you will get.'

Giving it some thought the first man wished that he could be in bed with the prettiest woman in the world. A swish was heard and he was gone.

'You might not believe this,' went on the second man, 'but as my wife was lost in the shipwreck, and as I always had a fancy for the sister-in-law . . . I wish that I could be with her right now.' Another swish was heard and he was gone.

'Now,' said the Genie, looking at the sad third man, 'what is your wish?'

'Well, I've been thinking it over,' he said, 'and I'm going to miss those two. So I wish that they were back here with me.'

A final swish was heard and the Genie disappeared, leaving three shipwrecked men sitting beside the sea on upturned barrels, just as they were before the Genie arrived.

714. Joe had worked all his life in the bowels of the earth as a miner, but modernisation and then recession had thrown him out of the pits and out of a job. He had just been to sort out details of his redundancy money and the amount quite pleased him. Wondering what to do with it, he decided to take the problem to the nearest pub.

Inside the pub he met up with a Chinese man, known ever since he entered this country as Sam Wan. Joe told Sam what had happened and that he was at a loose end, but was determined not to vegetate.

'Why not pool our money and open a chip shop here in town?' suggested Sam. He agreed to do the cooking if Joe looked after everything else.

A deal was arranged and a chip shop was set up and trade picked up immediately. Sam Wan did the cooking and Joe, being an early riser, travelled to the market every morning to pick up the fish.

It was the return leg of such a trip that put paid to their partnership, because one morning as Joe crossed the road with a box of fish a heavy lorry ran him down. Before he knew it he was drifting higher and higher, leaving cloud after cloud behind until he reached his new home of heaven. St Peter welcomed him at the gate and showed him around his new quarters.

After a few months St Peter sent for him and asked why it was that he looked so unhappy. Joe explained about how he had just set up shop with Sam Wan and was worried about leaving it to him to carry on the business.

St Peter instructed Joe to get a harp from the stores and make the journey back for a while, just to see if things were all right. So Joe took a harp from the stores and made the descent down to earth and was really surprised at what he saw. Sam had turned the chip shop into a disco and the place was bursting at the seams. Satisfied, Joe drifted through the disco before making his journey back.

He reported at once to St Peter and as this was heaven he had one confession to make. 'And what is that?' asked St Peter.

'You see . . .' Joe stumbled with the words. 'I left my harp in Sam Wan's disco!'

715. Squire Bandworth hadn't been feeling well lately and to see that his money and worldly goods were not pillaged by some unworthy relation he asked his solicitor for a copy of his will which he would read out to his staff so that they would know what to expect.

The staff assembled in the hallway opposite the study door and each was called in in turn. The butler was called in first, whilst the other staff pressed their ears to the door.

'Come in, Jarvis,' the Squire said. 'I suppose that you all know what this is about?' Jarvis nodded. 'You have looked after me, Jarvis, splendidly, for the last 30 years. No-one could have wished for a better butler. For that, Jarvis, I am about to leave you this house, Bandworth Hall, with 300 rooms, plus £300,000.' Jarvis went limp at the knees. 'Now send in the cook.'

'Good morning, Mrs Lucas. A splendid breakfast this morning, as usual,' he told the plump lady standing before him. The staff outside pressed their ears closer to the door. 'As you know, I love good food and you have given it to me. For that,' went on the Squire, moving his finger along the will, 'I am leaving you my country house, Bramble Hall, with its 200 rooms, plus £200,000.'

Mrs Lucas almost fainted as she made it to the door. Shamus O'Rourke, the gardener, pushed past her and stood before his master.

Squire Bandworth looked up. 'Ah, O'Rourke. What can I say about you? You've ruined the prize rose that had been bred by my late father. You ignored any instruction about the garden that I gave you. Yes, O'Rourke . . .' the Squire fidgeted in his seat, 'and for

157

that I am going to leave you sod all!'

O'Rourke seemed to relish the announcement. 'Sod Hall,' he mumbled. 'And could I ask how many rooms it has?'

716. The bells of Notre Dame were silent on this cold November morning which was quite surprising because Quasimodo hadn't failed to keep them ringing for what seemed like half a century. People looked at each other, wondering what was wrong, until Esmeralda appeared to hand a sick note to the priest. 'Quasimodo can't come to work this morning,' she whimpered, 'he's got a bad back.'

717. A hitman named Arty was bragging in his pub that he would take on any job for a pound. Overhearing this a shady looking character sidled up beside him at the bar and asked if the offer included murder.

On being told that his offer included anything and if that anything included murder then he was prepared to do it, the stranger produced a photograph from his pocket of a man and woman and passed it across to Arty with the one pound piece as payment. 'They attend the supermarket down the road every Thursday,' he told Arty.

A nod of the head and the deal was sealed.

A week went by without anything being brought to the man's attention until he walked into the bus station and read the headlines of the Evening Edition: 'ARTY CHOKES TWO FOR A POUND AT SUPERMARKET.'

718. Farmer Smith has just invented a new device which enables him to count his cows in the field quickly. He calls his invention a cowculator.

719. Richard was not very frightened when he saw the ghost and, since it appeared to be friendly, he asked the ghost if he could try to photograph it.

The ghost willingly agreed, and Richard went to fetch his camera, but found that the flash attachment on it was broken.

The spirit was willing – but the flash was weak.

720. I went round replacing every window in the house, then discovered I'd got a crack in my glasses.

721. My neighbour is the laziest man I know. He's so lazy that he married a pregnant woman!

POLITICS

722. A lifelong Labour supporter was lying, dying, on his bed when he suddenly decided to join the Tory party.

'But why?' asked his puzzled friends. 'You've been staunch Labour all your life.'

'Well,' said the dying man, 'I'd rather it was one of them that died than one of us.'

723. It was in the days of old when the man came riding into the noble's castle at great speed. As soon as his horse had entered the inner courtyard of the castle, the man leapt off his horse and ran into the noble's reception room.

'Sire! Sire! I and my men have done as you wished and raped and pillaged in the North.'

'Fool!' snapped the noble. 'I told you to rape and pillage in the West. I have no enemies in the North.'

'Sire!' replied the man. 'You do now!'

724. Two farm workers were discussing politics. Said one: 'I believe in the "share and share alike" policy. I think that we should all be equal.'

'Well,' replied the other, 'I don't know about that. Do you mean to say that if you had two horses you would give me one?'

'Certainly I would,' answered the first man.

'And,' went on the other, 'if you had two cars, would you give me one?'

'Of course,' came the reply.

'And,' said the other again, 'if you had two pigs, would you give me one?'

'Ah, now, wait a bit,' said the first man. 'You *know* that I've *got* two pigs!'

725. A new MP took his seat in the House of Commons today – but he was forced to put it back.

726. It is no use telling politicians to go to hell – they are trying to build it for us now.

727. You can always tell when politicians are lying – their lips move.

QUESTIONS

728. 'Now, how much would *you* like to contribute to the Indian Relief Fund, Mrs Custer?'

729. What do cannibals eat for breakfast? Buttered host.

730. How do you tell the sex of a hormone? Take its genes off.

731. 'What do you think about bathing beauties?'
  'I don't know – I've never bathed any.'

732. 'Do you write with your left hand or your right hand?
  'Neither – I write with a ballpoint pen.'

733. What goes 'tick, tock, woof'? A watch dog.

734. What goes 'zub, zub'? A bee flying backwards.

735. You know my rustproof, elephantproof, shock-proof, waterproof watch? Well, it just caught fire.

736. 'Where's Ruth?'
  'She's abroad.'
  'I asked *where* she was, not *what* she was.'

737. Simon: 'How do you make an elephant fly?'
  Clara: 'Use a very large zip.'

738. What is one of the main causes of sleepwalking? Twin beds.

739. 'That's a nice suit you're wearing – who went for the fitting?'

740. 'Do you smoke after making love?'
  'I don't know, I've never looked.'

741. Why do witches fly around on broomsticks?
  Because vacuum cleaners are too noisy.

742. What was the campaign slogan of dinosaurs

millions of years ago? Things will be better come the evolution.

743. 'Are you trying to make a fool out of me?'
'Of course not! Why should I try to change Nature?'

744. What is worse than when it's raining cats and dogs? When it's hailing taxis.

745. 'Apart from *that*, Mrs Lincoln, how did you enjoy the play?'

746. What do you call an Eskimo wearing five bala-clavas? Anything you like, because he can't hear you.

747. Whilst cleaning out the attic I found a piece of plastic with a hole in the middle. Is this a record?

748. 'Knock, knock.'
'Who's there?'
'Adolf.'
'Adolf who?'
'A dolf ball hid me in der moud and dat's why I talk fuddy.'

749. 'Are you enjoying yourself?'
'Yes, of course – what else is there to enjoy?'

750. 'Are you going to take a bath?'
'No – I'm going to leave it where it is.'

751. 'Did you know that deep breathing kills germs?'
'Yes. But how do you get them to breathe deeply?'

752. If you can't repeat gossip – what else can you do with it?

753. 'Which of your relations do you like best?'

'Sex.'

754. 'Why did you push him under a steamroller?'
'Because I wanted a flat mate.'

755. Did the coroner who lost his pub go on an inn quest?

756. If you sat in a bucket of glue would you have a sticky end?

757. 'Why are you jumping up and down?'
'Because I've just taken some medicine and I forgot to shake the bottle.'

758. Who was Joan of Arc? Noah's wife!

759. Where was Ann Boleyn beheaded? Just below the chin.

760. What's a hospice? About 3 gallons.

761. What happens when you immerse the human body in water?
The telephone rings.

762. Does fishing result in net profits?

763. 'Why are you drinking red and white paint?'
'Because I'm an interior decorator.'

764. Is playing tennis courting disaster – or is it a racket?

765. Is a budget a baby budgerigar?

766. 'What is fire?'
'That is a burning question.'

767. What did the policeman say to his stomach?
I've got you under a vest.

768. What is the opposite of minimum? Minidad.

769. At what battle did Nelson die? His last one.

770. What goes up bell ropes and is wrapped in a polythene bag? The lunchpack of Notre Dame.

771. What tables can you eat? Vegetables.

772. What is the difference between unlawful and illegal? Unlawful is against the law. Illegal is a sick bird.

773. What do you call a man who breaks into a house and steals ham? A ham burglar.

774. What was soft, sang and used to clean windows? Shammy Davis Jnr.

775. What is above a Rear Admiral? His hat.

776. What is smooth, round and green and conquered the world? Alexander the Grape!

777. What was the first thing Henry III did on coming to the throne? He sat down.

778. What is sticky and used to sing? Gluey Armstrong.

779. Why do storks only lift one leg? Because if they lifted the other leg they'd fall over.

780. What is hairy and coughs? A coconut with a cold.

781. What is the word with four letters, which ends

with 'k' and is another word for 'intercourse'? Talk.

782. If you suddenly heard a tap on the door would you immediately suspect a mad plumber?

783. What do you get when you cross some grass seed with a cow? A lawn moo-er.

784. What's afoot? The thing connected to your ankle.

785. Where do you take a sick horse? To the horse-pital.

786. How do you defeat someone? Chop off everything below their ankles.

787. What is wet, black, floats on water and shouts 'Knickers!'? Crude oil.

788. What is wet, black, floats on water and whispers 'Undergarments'? Refined oil.

789. If a plug would not fit, would you socket?

790. What do you do when your nose goes on strike? Picket.

791. Have you heard the story about the giant gate? You'll never get over it.

792. What do rich turtles wear? People-necked sweaters.

793. What is the last thing you take off before going to bed? Your feet off the floor.

794. Is the Privy Seal a creature with flippers kept in a privy?

795. Why do bees have sticky hair? Because they use honey combs.

796. What do you call a very large animal which keeps taking pills? A hippo-chondriac.

797. Do manufacturers of rope have all their assets tied up?

798. Why can't a bicycle stand up? Because it's two tyred.

799. If an artist becomes angry does he lose his tempera?

800. What is the favourite food of hedgehogs? Prickled onions.

801. Is a drunken ghost a methylated spirit?

802. Which side is it best to have the handle of a teacup on? The outside.

803. Do Arabs dance sheik to sheik?

804. Where was the Declaration of Independence signed? At the bottom.

805. Have you heard the joke about quicksand? It takes a long time to sink in.

806. What is furry, crunchy, and makes a noise when you pour milk on it? Mice crispies.

807. Where do you find mangoes? Where womangoes.

808. Do farmers take pig sties for grunted?

809. They are putting a clock on the leaning tower of Pisa. The Mayor said: 'What's the good of having the inclination if you haven't got the time?'

RELIGION

810. The village priest was passing Pat's cottage on Friday when he smelt something savoury frying, and looking in he saw Pat frying a pan of sausages.

'Why, Pat,' he said, 'what's this? Meat, and on a Friday! You must do penance. Bring me a load of wood tomorrow.'

Next day, Pat brought the load, but of sawdust.

'What's this?' said the priest, when he saw it. 'I said a load of wood.'

'Well,' said Pat, 'if sausages is meat, then sawdust is wood.'

811. A bishop was walking through a monastic garden and, looking around at all the trees and flowers, exclaimed: 'Oh, how wonderful are the works of the Lord!'

One of the gardeners, an old monk, on his knees at work, replied: 'But you should have seen it when He had it to Himself.'

812. In our small village the vicar has asked us for money for repairs to the church, a new church hall, new hymn books, and so many other causes that we're now known not as his flock, but as the fleeced.

813. Four-year-old James came home from a visit to the local church with his aunt and told his mother: 'I was very good and didn't give in to temptation. When they brought round a huge plate with money on it I said I didn't want it.'

814. A very attractive young girl was about to enter the church in a topless dress when the vicar ran towards her.

'I'm very sorry, madam,' said the vicar, 'but I cannot possibly allow you to go into Church like that.'

'But I have a divine right,' protested the young girl.

'Yes,' agreed the vicar, 'and you have a divine left too, but I still cannot let you into my church like that.'

815. A clergyman who stuttered and had spent many years abroad as a missionary was asked what had sustained him most in his work. He replied: 'My wife. She has b-b-been a big b-boon to me.'

816. Annette: 'Why do you keep diving down into the sea with signposts?'

Missionary: 'Because I'm trying to save a few more lost soles.'

817. A Roman Catholic priest, anxious to be friends with his counterparts in the Church of Scotland, invited a neighbouring minister to have tea at his house.

When the minister arrived, he was shown into a tastefully furnished drawing room, with a fitted carpet, soft and comfortable chairs, and fine pictures on the walls.

'My goodness,' declared the visiting minister. 'You priests certainly do yourselves well.'

The priest smiled. 'Ah, yes,' he nodded. 'You may have the better halves, my friend – but we have the better quarters.'

818. The tea manufacturers wanted a new advertising gimmick, so the senior creative man at their advertising agency decided to go to Rome to see if he could persuade the Pope to make a TV commercial.

The Pope gave the ad man an audience and he made his request. 'We'll give you £100,000 for a ten second commercial. All you have to do is say: "Give us this day our daily tea".'

'I'm sorry,' replied the Pope, 'but I cannot do as you request.'

'£500,000,' offered the ad man.

'I'm afraid not,' said the Pope, solemnly.

'All right, £1,000,000. And that's our very last offer.'

But still the Pope refused to make the commercial and the ad man left. On the way home the ad man turned to his secretary and said: 'That's odd. I mean, the Pope refusing to do a commercial for tea. I wonder how much the bread people are giving him.'

819. An Englishman and a Jew were talking about the ways of their respective races.

'You people,' said the Jew, 'have been taking things from us for thousands of years. The Ten Commandments, for instance.'

'Well, yes,' said the other, 'we took them from you all right, but you can't say that we've kept them.'

820. It was the little English girl's first visit to a church in the USA.

The clergyman was an extremely energetic preacher and during this sermon he stood in the pulpit and gestured wildly with his hands, shouted and wailed at his congregation, cajoled them, thumped the sides of the pulpit with his fists to emphasize certain points, and his facial expressions ranged from rage to kindness but all with extreme emotive passion.

As the clergyman stamped his feet and banged on his pulpit again, the little girl turned to her mother and whispered: 'I hope they keep him locked up in that little box – I wouldn't like to be near him if he gets out.'

821. A clergyman, who was summoned in haste by a woman taken ill suddenly, answered the call though somewhat puzzled, for he knew that she was not of his parish, and was, moreover, known to be a devoted worker in another church. While he was waiting to be shown to the sickroom he fell to talking to the little girl of the house.

'It is very gratifying to know that your mother thought of me in her illness,' he said. 'Is your own minister out of town?'

'Oh, no,' answered the child in a matter of fact tone, 'he's home. Only we thought it might be something contagious – and we didn't want to take any risks.'

822. 'Next week,' said the vicar, 'my sermon will be entirely about truthfulness and I think it is especially important that on getting home from church today – or at least some time during the week – that you read the twenty-ninth chapter of Leviticus.'

The following week the vicar started his sermon: 'Last week I said that my sermon this week would be about truthfulness and I asked you all to read the twenty-ninth chapter of Leviticus. Now, can all those who did this please raise their right hands.'

Almost the entire congregation raised their right hands.

'Just as I suspected!' said the vicar. 'And that is why my sermon today is about truthfulness. You could not possibly have read the twenty-ninth chapter of Leviticus. Leviticus only has twenty-seven chapters!'

823. A parson remarked to one of his church wardens: 'Have you noticed that, after the service, many of the men in the choir cross over to the local inn?'

'Oh, yes,' replied the church warden. 'I expect it's the thirst after righteousness.'

824. Two curates were talking. One said: 'How do you get on with the young ladies in your parish?'

The other replied: 'I seek safety in numbers. How about you?'

The first curate answered: 'I take refuge in exodus.'

825. A little girl, a vicar's daughter, saw a bishop in all his robes for the first time. She gazed at him in wonder for a moment, then smoothing the handsome stole that he was wearing said: 'And have you panties to match?'

826. A new piece of carpet had been put on the floor of the pulpit and the vicar noticed some tacks scattered around.

'James,' he said to the verger, 'whatever would happen if I trod on one of these tacks during my sermon?'

'Well,' replied the verger. 'I reckon that would be one point that you wouldn't linger on.'

827. A parson, who could find no place to park his car, wrote a little note which he stuck on the windscreen, stating: 'I have searched high and low for a place to park without success – Forgive us our trespasses.'

A policeman who spotted him also wrote a little note: 'The Sergeant will be around in five minutes – Lead us not into temptation.'

828. The rabbi and the priest lived next door to each other and bought new cars almost exactly at the same time.

Looking out of his window, the rabbi saw the priest with a small bowl of water sprinkling the contents over the car and blessing it.

Not to be outdone, the rabbi got a hacksaw and cut

half an inch off the exhaust pipe of his own car.

829. 'My Catholic priest knows more than your Methodist minister,' said ten-year-old Nathan.

'Of course he does,' replied David. 'You have to tell him everything.'

830. One tribe of cannibals were converted by missionaries to becoming good Catholics – they ate fishermen only on Fridays.

831. Two little girls were discussing their respective families. 'Why does your grandmother read her Bible so much?' asked one.

The other replied: 'I think she's cramming for her finals.'

832. Old lady to vicar who is leaving the parish: 'I'm sorry you're going, Vicar. We never knew what sin was until you came.'

833. A woman was sending an old family Bible through the post. As she presented the parcel at the Post Office counter she was asked: 'Anything breakable?'

'Well, no,' she replied. 'Nothing but the Ten Commandments.'

834. Candida was eighty years old and one day she went to confession and said: 'Father, I have sinned. I have committed adultery with a seventeen-year-old gardener.'

'When was this?' asked the priest.

'Fifty years ago – but I just felt like recalling pleasant experiences this week.'

835. 'Mummy,' asked a little girl, 'do men ever go to heaven?'

'Why, yes, of course, dear,' answered her mother.

'Why do you ask?'

'Because I've never seen angels with whiskers.'

'Well,' replied the mother, 'some men do go to heaven, but they only get there by a close shave.'

836. Rabbi Cohen and Father O'Connor were at a party when they were each offered a ham sandwich.

Rabbi Cohen declined the sandwich, and the Catholic priest chided him: 'Come, come, rabbi – when are you going to become liberal enough to eat ham?'

The rabbi smiled and replied: 'At your wedding, Father O'Connor.'

837. A clergyman named Jordan had a son at college. The son was about to take his final examinations and naturally the father asked the boy to let him know as soon as possible how he got on.

One day the father received a telegram which read: 'Hymn 254, verse five, last two lines.'

Looking up the reference in the hymn book, he read: 'Sorrow vanquished, labour ended, Jordan passed.'

838. During a conversation with a kindly old priest, the young man asked: 'Is it really such a sin to sleep with a girl?'

'Oh, no,' replied the priest, 'but you young men – you don't sleep.'

839. 'Hello! Is that the Salvation Army?'

'Yes, it is.'

'Is it true that you save fallen girls?'

'Yes.'

'Then will you save one for me for Thursday night?'

840. Two clergymen were talking and one said, 'Do you know, I dread having to preach a long sermon, for one or two members of my congregation have the habit of looking at their watches. One cannot help noticing and it puts me off.'

The other replied: 'Oh, I never mind if they look at their watches. It's when they hold them to their ears as though they had stopped that I find discouraging.'

841. Vicar: 'You know, I pray for you every night.'

Young woman: 'Well, there's really no need – I *am* on the phone.'

842. 'My wife is an Eighth Day Adventist.'

'Don't you mean a Seventh Day Adventist?'

'No – she's always late for everything.'

843. 'Now, what have we got to do before we can get forgiveness of sin?'

'Sin?'

844. One clergyman had a flashing orange nose, so he was known as the Belisha Deacon.

845. Is the Chief Rabbi of the Eskimos called Eskimoses?

846. A little girl's prayer: 'Oh, God, make the bad people good, and the good people nice.'

847. A clergyman wrote to his bishop as follows: 'I regret to inform you, my lord, but my wife has died. Could you please send me a substitute for the weekend?'

848. A clergyman and one of his elderly parishioners were walking home from church one frosty day when the old gentleman slipped and fell flat on his back. The minister looked at him for a moment, and being assured that he was not hurt, said: 'Friend, sinners stand on slippery places.'

The old gentleman looked up at him and said: 'I see

they do, but I can't.'

849. One Sunday morning a minister had been telling his congregation that there was a sermon in every blade of grass. The following day, when he was cutting his grass in the vicarage garden, a parishioner who was passing called out: 'That's right, Vicar. Keep them short.'

850. A farmer invited the new minister to lunch one Sunday. Together they sat down to partake of a nice roast chicken.

Afterwards, as they sat at the window with their coffee, the visitor pointed to a fine rooster which strutted across the farmyard. 'My word,' he said, 'but that's a proud bird you've got there and no mistake.'

The farmer replied with a smile: 'He should be proud, indeed. After all, one of his sons has just entered the ministry.'

851. It was Christmas morning and the family were plodding home from church through the snow, discussing the service. They all seemed to have a bad word to say.

Dad thought the bells had been rung dreadfully; Mum thought the hymns were badly chosen; the eldest son fell asleep during the sermon and his twin sister could not agree with the prayers. All except for the youngest boy who said: 'I don't know what you are all complaining about; *I* thought it was a damn good show for 10p!'

852. An ancient Japanese General and an old British Major were talking.

'Why do you always win battles, whereas we always seem to lose all our wars, except the economic ones?' asked the Japanese General.

'Because we always pray to God before we go into

battle,' replied the British Major.

'That's not so, because we also pray to God – but we never win.'

'Ah!' said the British Major, 'but not everyone can understand Japanese.'

853. The local vicar was invited to do an after dinner speech because he was well known in the area for offering more than one humorous tale.

Noting a goodly number of reporters in the audience, and knowing that he could dine regularly on the same stories time and again, he decided to have a word with them and ask them not to repeat his coveted stories.

To his amazement, the following day all the papers said: 'The vicar told stories we are unable to print.'

854. It was Mothering Sunday and a young curate who was to preach mounted the pulpit and said: 'Instead of starting my sermon with a text, I shall give you a toast instead.' He then went on: 'Here's to the happiest days of my life, spent in the arms of another man's wife – my mother.' And a very appropriate sermon for the occasion followed.

Now, a bishop who was on holiday was in the congregation and he thought to himself, 'That's a good introduction, I must remember that.' Shortly afterwards, the opportunity presented itself, and he started off his sermon with the toast, saying: 'Here's to the happiest days of my life, spent in the arms of another man's wife . . .' and then his memory failed him and he said: 'Now whatever was the lady's name?'

855. Another young curate went to a conference at which most of the gathering consisted of bishops, archdeacons and other high dignitaries of the church. The weather was cold and it was natural perhaps that the old clergy should cluster round the cheerful fire in the dining room as often as possible.

The curate thought that it was about time that he did something about this, so next morning he said in a loud voice: 'I had a rather strange dream last night. I dreamt that I had died and gone to hell.'

After a few moments of dead silence one of the number said: 'And what did you find there?'

'Just the same as here,' came the reply. 'I couldn't get near the fire for bishops.'

856. A rather stone-faced and cold, celibate clergyman died and, soon after, one of his best friends also passed away.

On arriving in the 'other place' the clergyman's friend was surprised to see the clergyman with two beautiful blonde ladies sitting on his knee, and a gorgeous black-haired lady stroking his shoulders. All three were clearly trying to seduce him.

'I see you're being well treated,' said the friend. 'I didn't realize Heaven was going to be so good.'

'I'm not enjoying myself,' replied the clergyman with a sour look. 'And this isn't Heaven. We're in Hell – and I'm these three ladies' punishment.'

857. Abe rushed round to Samuel's house, extremely distressed. 'The most terrible thing has just happened. I met my son off the plane this morning and he says to me: "Papa," he says, "I've been converted. I'm a Christian."'

Samuel listened in silence, then said, quietly: 'Well, the same thing happened to me. I, too, just met my son off the ship and he too has been converted. What shall we do?'

They decided to consult the rabbi but, alas, his son had suddenly been converted too. So, in desperation, the three men went to the synagogue and prayed as they had never prayed before.

After a while there was a great crash of thunder and a voice boomed: 'Gentlemen, you know what? I had the same trouble myself!'

858. Vicar: 'Now tell me, Freda. How many times a day do you say prayers?'

Four-year-old Freda: 'Once, sir. At night.'

Vicar: 'But don't you say any prayers at all during the day?'

Freda: 'No, sir. I'm only frightened at night.'

859. An old Irish woman visited Lourdes and on her return journey, as she passed through Customs, there was a black bottle discovered in her luggage.

'What's in this bottle?' asked the Customs Officer.

'Sure, 'tis just some holy water,' came the reply.

'I shall have to test it,' said the officer and he unscrewed the stopper and sniffed the contents. 'Why,' he said, 'this isn't water, it's whisky!'

'Praise be to God!' cried the old lady. ' 'Tis indeed a holy miracle!'

860. A vicar called Mark was closing the church doors after an evening service when he heard a strange voice call: 'Mark! Mark!'

He looked outside the church, but could find no one calling his name. Then he looked inside the Church, but although the voice still called 'Mark! Mark!' the poor clergyman could not find where the sounds were coming from.

Finally, he rushed to the altar, thinking it must be God calling him. But when he got there all he found was a dog with a hare lip.

861. A train was journeying through the night and down the corridor went an American, calling out: 'Is there a Roman Catholic priest on the train?'

Meeting with no response, he retraced his steps, calling out this time: 'Is there an English Catholic priest on the train?'

He had almost reached the last carriage when a little man wearing a dog collar stepped out into the corridor and said: 'Excuse me, I heard you asking first for a Roman Catholic priest and then for an English Catholic priest. Can I be of any help? I'm a Nonconformist Minister.'

'Not a hope in hell,' came the reply. 'I'm only trying to borrow a corkscrew!'

862. A vicar's wife asked her children what they were doing in their father's study. 'It's a great secret, Mummy,' they replied. 'We're giving Daddy a new Bible for his birthday and we thought that we'd better copy what Daddy's friends put in the books they give him. So we're writing "With the author's compliments".'

863. A Scotsman died and arrived outside Heaven's gates.

'Who is there?' cried a voice.

'Sandy McTavish,' replied the Scot.

'I'm sorry,' the voice said, 'you'll have to go to the other place, we can't make porridge for one!'

864. The Lord prefers common looking people. That's why he made so many of us.

865. At a dinner a very pompous American woman was seated next to a rabbi. Wishing to impress him she said rather grandly: 'One of my ancestors signed the Declaration of Independence.'

'Indeed?' replied the rabbi. 'One of mine wrote the Ten Commandments.'

866. Eric was making one of his rare visits to church and had much to talk to his priest about. For 40 minutes he had sat before the confession box, pouring out his heart about all the bad habits and mis-dealings that he had drifted into.

Suddenly the confession box door opened and out stepped the cleaner.

'You haven't been in there for the last 40 minutes?' asked Eric, looking uncomfortable. The cleaner nodded.

'But I thought I was talking to Father Mason,' he went on.

'By what *I* have heard in the last 40 minutes,' said the cleaner, 'you would be better off talking to Perry Mason!'

867. In an Irish village there was an English Catholic priest and an Irish Catholic priest. Pat, one of the villagers, had some kittens for disposal so he went along to the English Catholic priest and offered him the choice saying: 'They're the finest English Catholic kittens.' But the priest wasn't having any of his blarney and refused.

Pat then approached the Irish Catholic priest and offered them to him, saying this time: 'Sure, they're the finest Irish Catholic kittens you could ever wish to see.'

But in the meantime the two priests had conferred together, so the Irish Catholic priest said: 'But, Pat, I heard that you described these kittens as the finest English Catholic kittens.'

'Well,' said Pat, 'sure I did. But that was nine days ago, and haven't they had their eyes opened since?'

868. Definition of circumcision: that which cuts off the Jews from the Gentiles.

869. Adam was the world's first book-keeper. He turned over a leaf and made an entry.

870. The wages of sin are high – unless you know someone who'll do it for free.

871. It was the old missionary in Africa who gave the

180

tribe of cannibals their first taste of Christianity.

872. Late in the 19th century, a Nativity play was to be performed in the Church Hall and a country vicar went to town to get a streamer for display. Unfortunately he forgot the measurements so he wired his wife for details. The telegraph clerk at the other end nearly had a fit when this reply message was received. It read: 'Unto us a Child is Born – seven feet six by one foot three.'

873. The vicar was explaining the difference between knowledge and faith to his congregation.

'In the front row,' he said, 'we have Mr Heather with his wife and three children. Now, she *knows* they are her children – that's knowledge. He *believes* they are his children – that's faith.'

874. A clergyman had cause to reprove one of his parishioners who unfortunately lost his temper and as a parting shot shouted out: 'If I had an imbecile son I would put him in the Church.'

'Your father evidently thought differently,' replied the cleric meekly.

875. On John's first visit to Rome he got caught up in the crowds that thronged the Vatican and although it wasn't something he expected, he decided to join in with things when he heard that the Pope was going to move amongst the crowd.

Sure enough, the Pope made his appearance and made a bee line to a man whose neck seemed to be rigid. After the Pope touched his neck he was able to swing it about in all directions.

Further along a man sat squat with his leg twisted behind him, but after the Pope touched the limb the man danced about with excitement.

Slowly the Pope moved towards John, but as his

hand moved forward John recoiled in fear. 'No, no,' he cried out, 'don't touch me!'

'Why not?' asked the Pope, not believing what he had heard.

'You see, my Disablement Benefit Claim has only just been accepted!'

876. A large and portly clergyman was a visiting preacher at a small country church. Mounting the pulpit which creaked audibly under his weight he announced: 'I shall come down and dwell amongst you,' at the same time bringing his hands down with a resounding bang on the ledge.

The words of his text and the accompanying action he repeated twice more, so it was not surprising that on the third occasion the pulpit collapsed and the preacher and structure fell on the first two rows of pews.

As he clambered out of the wreckage, one elderly parishioner was heard to remark: 'Well, parson, I must say you gave us fair warning.'

877. A missionary went to a remote part of the world to teach some natives. On his travels he came to a small village where he decided to make a speech. It went something like this:

Missionary: 'All men are your enemies and you must love your enemies.'

The natives raised their spears and shouted: 'Hussanga!'

Missionary: 'If a man should smite you, turn the other cheek.'

The natives raised their spears again and shouted: 'Hussanga!'

Missionary: 'Fighting is wrong – you must not fight.'

Once again, the natives raised their spears and shouted: 'Hussanga!'

The missionary decided he had said enough for one day, and as he made his way off the platform he said to the native nearest to him: 'I think my little speech went down quite well, don't you? You all seemed to agree with it.'

'Hmmm,' said the native. 'Mind you don't tread in the hussanga when you get off the platform.'

878. Two British sailors attended a church service in Stockholm. Not wishing to appear out of place they sat behind an important looking man and when he stood up or knelt down, they did the same. At the end of the service, the pastor made what was evidently an announcement, whereupon the man in front of the sailors rose to his feet, and they did likewise – to a roar of laughter from the congregation.

As the sailors left the church, the pastor spoke to them in English, so they asked him the reason for the laughter. 'Oh!' he said, 'I mentioned that next Sunday morning there was to be a baptism and would the father of the child please stand up.'

879. Three clergyman – an English priest, an Irish priest and a Scots minister – were attending a conference in Scotland for church unity. At the conclusion they decided to go for a day's fishing in the nearby loch and having hired a boat, set off and anchored a little way from the shore. They were having good luck with the fishing when suddenly the line of the Scots minister was fouled and, having no other of that particular tackle available, he decided to go ashore to get some more. Going down on his knees in the bow of the boat, he prayed very earnestly and then, stepping over the side, walked across the surface of the water to the shore, returning in like manner.

A little later the English priest had need to go ashore and he also knelt down and prayed and then stepped over the side of the boat and walked over the water, returning in due course.

Presently, it was found that their supplies were

running short so the first two clergymen looked at the Irish priest who said that he would go ashore to bring back replenishments. He also knelt and prayed and then stepped over the side of the boat as his companions had done previously. But he went right down in the water, and as the other two clergymen watched him sink one said to the other: 'Perhaps for the sake of Christian unity we should have pointed out where the stepping stones were!'

880. Three Englishmen were on vacation to the Vatican and after an early morning stroll headed back to their hotel, only to find that a man had dropped dead on the hotel steps.

'It's the Pope!' shouted one of the men, before running into the hotel to give the alarm.

The three men were kept under strict security until the heads of the Vatican were called who immediately called a meeting amongst themselves. The leader of the group addressed the three men: 'We don't want to release this news for a full week in order to prepare the world for such a sad occurrence,' he said. 'And we would like a promise from you three that you will keep our secret.' All three men nodded their heads.

On the aircraft the next day, one of the men had a brainwave: 'I know how we can make a sure profit from this without breaking our word.' The other two were interested and wanted to know how.

'If we go to the betting shop and ask what odds they would give that the Pope died this week, we could make a bundle!' On this they all agreed.

The following week the three men met again.

'I told you,' said the first man. 'I withdrew all my savings and got odds of a thousand to one.'

The second man gulped. 'I wasn't quite that lucky, but I got a smashing bet placed at nine hundred to one.' He stroked the bulge in his pocket. 'And how did you get on?' he asked the third man, who wasn't very bright and looked sad.

'I lost,' he stammered.

'You lost?' his friends asked in unison. 'How could you lose? It was a sure thing!'

'You see . . .' he answered, casting his eyes to the ground, 'I backed it as a double with the Archbishop of Canterbury.'

RESTAURANTS/FOOD

881. I once worked as a chef in a restaurant that only served food to midgets. In fact, I was a short order cook.

882. 'Waiter, can I have some undercooked chips, some gooey, cold beans and a fried egg coated in old grease?'

'I'm sorry, sir, but we couldn't possibly give you anything like that.'

'Why not? That's what you gave me yesterday.'

883. An irate customer followed a man to the bar who had been sitting at the next table.

'Excuse me,' said the irate customer, 'but you broke wind before my wife.'

'I'm dreadfully sorry,' said the man. 'I didn't know that we were taking turns.'

884. Waiter: 'What would madam like for dessert?'

Customer: 'An assortment of real cream ice cream – say, two scoops of chocolate chip, one scoop of vanilla, three scoops of banana, two scoops of strawberry and please cover the lot with thick chocolate sauce.'

Waiter: 'Certainly, madam. And would you like a

few cherries on the top?'
    Customer: 'No thank you. I'm on a diet.'

885. The loud-mouthed American from Mobile, Alabama, was in the coffee shop of an expensive hotel in London.

'How would you like your coffee, sir?' inquired a waiter.

'I like my coffee just like my women – strong and sweet,' replied the American.

'Quite sir,' said the waiter. 'Black or white?'

886. A man was amazed to find a restaurant advertising: 'Chicken dinners – only 90p.'

He decided to try one of these dinners so he paid his 90p and his taste buds began to anticipate the pleasant chicken dinner that was to come – until the waiter brought him a plate of corn.

887. Spinster: 'So the waiter says to me, how would you like your rice?'

Friend: 'Yes, dearie, go on.'

Spinster: 'So I says, wistfully, "Thrown at me".'

888. Customer: 'Why is this chop so terribly tough?'

Waiter: 'Because, sir, it's a karate chop.'

889. Waiter: 'Sir, would you like the chef's Surprise Pie?'

Customer: 'What's in it?'

Waiter: 'Chicken, sir.'

Customer: 'So what's the surprise?'

Waiter: 'The chef forgot to take the feathers off it.'

890. Waiter: 'Would you like something to eat?'

Customer who has waited forty-five minutes for service: 'No, thank you – I don't want to waste my lunch hour.'

891. Customer: 'Excuse me, but how long have you been working here?'

Waitress: 'About three months, sir.'

Customer: 'Oh. Then it couldn't have been you who took my order.'

892. A waiter in a top restaurant apologised to a regular customer as he handed out the menu. 'I want you to know,' he said, 'that the flaky pastry is not now on the menu. The chef's dermatitis has cleared up.'

893. 'Waiter! What is this stuff in the bowl?'

'It's bean soup, sir.'

'I don't want to know what it's been – what is it now?'

894. Waiter: 'What would you like, sir?'

Customer: 'Steak and chips.'

Waiter: 'Would you like anything with it, sir?'

Customer: 'If it's like the last one I ate here, then bring me a hammer and chisel.'

895. 'Waiter! This egg is bad.'

'Don't blame me, I only lay the table.'

896. Customer: 'Waiter! There's a worm on my plate.'

Waiter: 'That's not a worm, sir. That's your sausage.'

897. 'Waiter! What are these coins doing in my soup?'

'Well, sir, you said you would stop coming to this restaurant unless there was change in the meals.'

898. Customer: 'Have you got asparagus?'

Waiter: 'No, we don't serve sparrows and my name is *not* Gus.'

899. Another customer: 'Waiter, was that your handkerchief you wiped my plate with just now?'

Waiter: 'Oh, that's all right, sir. It's not a clean one.'

900. 'Waiter! Please bring me a coffee without cream.'

'I'm very sorry, madam, but we've run out of cream. Would you like it without milk instead?'

901. 'Waiter! Is this food pure?'

'As pure as the girl of your dreams, sir.'

'Oh! Then I'd rather not have it, thanks.'

902. The beautiful young girl was lying naked on the roof of her expensive hotel, sunbathing. Suddenly the manager came up to her, coughed slightly, then said: 'Excuse me, madam, but this is hardly the place for nudity.'

'Why not?' asked the girl. 'I can't see anyone.'

'That may be so,' replied the manager, 'but you are lying on the skylight over the dining room and it is now lunch time.'

903. An American tourist, visiting England, had just enjoyed a delicious dinner in a Winchester restaurant.

'Would you like coffee, sir?' inquired a waiter.

'Certainly,' replied the American.

'Cream or milk?'

'Neither,' said the American, firmly. 'Just give me what I'm used to back home: a pasteurized blend of water, corn syrup solids, vegetable oil, sodium casein-ate, carrageenan, guargum, disodium phosphate, poly-sorbate 60, sorbitan monostearate, potassium sorbate and artificial colour.'

904. Then there was the sadist who became a chef so he could whip cream and beat eggs.

905. Notice in a foreign hotel: 'The water in this establishment is completely hygienic – it has all been passed by the manager.'

906. Notice in the window of a health food restaurant:

'Our salad dinners will take your breadth away.'

907. The Tandoori restaurant owner was having complaints about how uncomfortable his curry was making his customers when they had to visit the loo, so he renamed his restaurant 'Shy Tot'.

908. 'Waiter! There's a fly in my soup.'
'Would you prefer it to be served separately?'

909. 'Waiter! There's a fly in my soup.'
'If you throw it a pea it'll play water polo.'

910. 'Waiter! There's a fly in my soup.'
'No sir, that's the chef. The last customer was a witch doctor.'

911. 'Waiter! There's a fly in my soup.'
'If you leave it there the goldfish will eat it.'

912. 'Waiter! There's a fly in my soup.'
'I know sir! It's fly soup.'

913. 'Waiter! There's a fly in my soup.'
'Oh, dear, it must have committed insecticide.'

914. 'Waiter! There's a fly in my soup.'
'I'm sorry, sir, the dog must have missed it.'

915. 'Waiter! There's a fly in my soup.'
'That's the meat, sir.'

916. 'Waiter! There's a fly in my soup.'
'It's the rotting meat that attracts them, sir.'

917. 'Waiter! How dare you splash soup on my trousers!'
'I'm sorry, sir, but now you've got soup in your fly.'

918. Customer at Chinese restaurant: 'Do you do take-aways?'

Owner: 'Yes. 10 from 15 is 5.'

919. 'Urrgh!' said Mr Blenkinsop, 'this lamb is tough.'

'I'm sorry,' replied his wife, but the butcher said it was a spring lamb.'

'Then that explains it,' said Mr Blenkinsop. 'I must be eating one of the springs.'

920. When I lived in lodgings my landlady kept some animals in the yard at the back of the house.

The first day I was there, one of the chickens died, so we had chicken soup.

The next day, the pig died, so I was offered pork chops.

The following day, the duck died, so we had roast duck with apple sauce.

The next day my landlady's husband died – so I left.

921. When things were rationed during the war the hostess at a small dinner party, turning to one of her guests, asked: 'Well, Mr Brown, and how did you find the meat?'

'Oh,' he replied, 'I just moved a potato and there it was.'

922. 'Quite honestly, Henrietta, I shall be glad when we've eaten the last of that rhinoceros . . .'

923. 'I've made the chicken soup.'

'Good! I was worried it was for us.'

924. Mavis: 'My doctor put me on a new diet, using more corn and other vegetable oils.'

Beryl: 'Does it work?'

Mavis: 'Well, I'm not any thinner yet – but I don't squeak any more.'

925. A party of countrymen had planned a trip to London, to see the Houses of Parliament, Buckingham Palace and other places of interest. They were all waiting in the coach except Old George who was late in arriving. At last he came puffing along carrying a large basket of plums.

'What have you got them for?' someone called out.

'They're for 'Er Majesty the Queen,' replied Old George. 'Don't it say in the National Anthem, "Send 'Er Victorias"?'

926. The posh dinner party had been a great success until, over coffee, one of the guests decided to tell a long and intimately detailed blue joke.

The host of the dinner party was appalled: 'That was an outrageous joke! How dare you tell such a story before my wife!'

'I'm sorry,' replied the joke teller, 'I didn't realise your wife wanted to tell it herself!'

927. A man called on a married couple whom he had not seen for some time. The door was opened by the woman to whom the man said: 'Hello, Mabel, and how is Jack?'

'Oh,' she replied, 'didn't you know? He died a little while ago.'

'Well, I am sorry to hear that,' the man said. 'How did it happen?'

'Well,' she informed him, 'he went into the garden to pull a cabbage for dinner, when he collapsed and died.'

'Dear, dear,' said the man, 'whatever did you do?'

'Well,' she rejoined, 'what could we do? We had to open a tin of peas.'

928. 'I've prepared the turkey,' said Charles proudly to his wife. 'I've plucked it and stuffed it. All you've got to do is kill it and cook it.'

ROMANCE/RELATIONSHIPS

929. My girlfriend used to kiss me on the lips – but it's all over now.

930. 1st girl: 'What would you give a man who has everything?'
2nd girl: 'Encouragement.'

931. Two ageing film actresses were walking along when one said: 'Do you know the best way to keep your youth?'
The other replied: 'Lock him in the bedroom.'

932. There had been a lover's quarrel and afterwards the mother said to her son: 'Why don't you and Sarah kiss and make up?'
'Oh, that's all right, Mother,' the son replied, 'we have kissed and Sarah's making-up now.'

933. My girlfriend was arrested in one of those conservative foreign countries for wearing a bikini top that was far too small, even though the policeman who arrested her agreed with me that she had two fantastic excuses.

934. Young man, turning to the girl seated next to him: 'You know, Jenny,' he said, 'your parents have invited me to dinner so often I'm beginning to feel sort of obligated. Will you marry me?'

935. 'Mummy,' said little Jimmy, 'I want to live with Carol next door.'

'But you're both only six years old,' smiled his mother. 'Where will you live?'

'In her bedroom.'

'What will you live off? You don't have any money – and what will you do if babies come along?'

'Well,' said Jimmy, seriously, 'we've been all right so far . . . and if she lays any eggs then I'll tread on them!'

936. After going into Hazel Wood with his girlfriend, a disappointed Fred came out and wrote under the sign which said 'Hazel Wood' the words: 'but Janice wouldn't.'

937. Henry used to go out with a girl who was very class conscious. He didn't have any class and she was very conscious of it.

938. A rather diminutive army officer attended the regimental dance. Arriving late, he saw that everyone was dancing with the exception of one woman. Going up to her and bowing, he said: 'May I have the pleasure of this dance?'

Looking him up and down she replied somewhat haughtily: 'I don't dance with a child.'

Quick as a flash he retorted: 'I am sorry madam, I was not aware of your condition.'

939. The couple were on a pre-honeymoon cruise when suddenly a storm blew up and their ship was smashed to pieces by the powerful waves.

Clinging to a plank of wood, the couple managed to survive in the sea for two days without food or water.

On the third day, the man began to pray even more frantically than before: 'Oh, dear Lord, please save us. Please – we beg you to spare our lives and make us safe and end our misery in this cruel sea. Please – if you save us I promise to give up the sins of gambling, smoking, swearing, drinking, and I will refrain from . . .'

He was interrupted by his girlfriend, who said: 'Better stop there – I think we're approaching land!'

940. The small car pulled up to a sudden halt. 'Have you run out of petrol?' asked the girl, somewhat sarcastically.

'No, of course not,' replied her young male companion.

'Then why have we stopped?'

'You will no doubt have noticed that we are parked in a secluded spot in the middle of this forest and miles from anywhere – so I thought you might like a discussion about the hereafter.'

'That's something new,' replied the young girl. 'What do you mean?'

'Simple! If you're not hereafter what I'm hereafter, you'll be hereafter I've gone.'

941. A fellow said to a friend: 'Could I ask your advice on a rather important matter, old boy?'

'Certainly,' came the reply.

'Well, it's like this. I'm in love with two girls, that is, I think I am. Now, one is very beautiful but has no money, while the other is rather nice but very plain although she is rolling. What would you do in the circumstances?'

'Well,' said the friend, 'I'm sure that in your heart you love the beautiful one, so I should go ahead and marry her.'

'Right!' said the fellow. 'That's what I'll do.'

As he prepared to depart, the friend said: 'Oh, by the way, I wonder if you could give me the address of the other girl?'

942. It was in a nudist camp and the beautiful young woman walked over to the young man.

'Pleased to meet you,' said the man.

The girl looked down, blushed, and said: 'I can see you are.'

943. 'My dearest, sweetest, beautiful darling! Will you love me always?'

'Of course, darling. Which way do you want to try first?'

944. A young man was loudly lamenting to everyone in the bar that his doctor had ordered him to give up half his sex life.

'Which half are you going to give up?' asked a bored listener. 'Talking about it – or thinking about it?'

945. Adrian: 'Why do all the men find Victoria so attractive?'

Simon: 'Because of her speech impediment.'

Adrian: 'Her speech impediment?'

Simon: 'Yes. She can't say "no".'

946. Man: 'My sister married an Irishman.'

Friend: 'Oh, really?'

Man: 'No, O'Reilly.'

947. Man: 'Have you been to bed with anyone?'

Girl (angrily): 'That's *my* business!'

Man: 'Oh! I didn't know you were a professional.'

948. 'Say when, dear.'

'After the drinks, darling.'

949. She was only a police constable's daughter, but she let the detective inspector.

950. Girl: 'I'll pour the drinks. What will you have – gin and platonic?'

Young man: 'I was hoping for whisky and sofa.'

951. Judge: 'Did you sleep with this woman?'
Man in witness box: 'No, your honour, not a wink.'

952. 'Darling, you have the face of a saint.'
'Dearest, you say the sweetest things! Which saint?'
'A Saint Bernard!'

953. His girlfriend is so thin it takes three of her to make a shadow. Once when she swallowed a prune she was rushed to the maternity clinic.

954. 'Darling, what do you think of the Middle East position?'
'I don't know, I've never tried it.'

955. An old gentleman asked the pretty girl if she wanted to come up to his room to help him write his will.

956. John's new girlfriend thinks that oral contraception is when she talks her way out of it.

957. Man, snuggling up to girl: 'Am I the first man you ever made love to?'
Girl, pushing man back and looking at him carefully: 'You might be – your face looks familiar.'

958. The shy English girl on her first visit to Scotland nervously went up to a handsome young Scot who was wearing his national costume and asked: 'Excuse me speaking to a stranger, but I've always been curious. Please can you tell me what is worn under the kilt?'
The Scotsman smiled and said: 'Nothing is worn – everything is in excellent condition.'

959. Henry: 'My girlfriend and I want to get married in church, but do you approve of sex before marriage?'
Clergyman: 'If it delays the service – no!'

960. There is nothing so restful as the sleep of the just –
except, perhaps, the sleep of the just after.

961. Every girl that I took home my mother didn't like.
Blondes were too dirty for me, red heads were too
fiery, brunettes too flighty. I just couldn't please her.
One night I was in a dance hall when I met this girl who
was the spitting image of my mother in looks, ways,
speech and everything.

    I took her home and my dad didn't like her!

962. John could marry any girl he pleased – trouble is,
he didn't please any of them.

963. As the train thundered along, the man turned to
the woman in the otherwise deserted compartment and
said: 'Would you let me kiss you for fifty pence?'

    'Certainly not!' retorted the woman.

    The man returned to his newspaper.

    A few minutes later the man asked: 'Would you let
me kiss you for a thousand pounds?'

    'Yes,' replied the woman, after a brief pause.

    A few minutes later the man asked: 'Would you let
me kiss you for a pound?'

    'Certainly not!' exclaimed the woman. 'What kind of
a woman do you think I am?'

    'We've already established that. Now we're just
haggling over the price.'

964. 'My girlfriend says I'm handsome.'

    'That's only because you feed her guide dog.'

965. 'I've just got engaged,' said Sally, flashing her ring
around the typing pool.

    'Yes,' said one of her colleagues, Kathy. 'The person
who gave it to you is about six feet tall, has medium
length brown hair, blue eyes, and a small tattoo in the
shape of a butterfly on his right shoulder.'

'Fantastic, Sherlock Holmes!' exclaimed Sally. 'You can tell all that just by looking at the ring?'

'Certainly,' replied Kathy. 'It's the one I gave him back six months ago.'

966. The young man arrived late at night at a small hotel in a remote village in Scotland.

After a hot supper, the middle-aged owners of the hotel bade him goodnight, but warned him: 'Make sure you lock your bedroom door before going to sleep as our Stella walks in her sleep.'

The young man, with visions of a delicious young female named Stella sleep-walking into his room, made sure to leave his door open.

Two hours after falling asleep he was rudely awakened by a coarse tongue licking his face and a heavy weight on his chest and body. He opened his eyes to see Stella, the biggest sheepdog he'd ever seen.

967. A little old lady was busy making herself some tea one afternoon when a fairy appeared in her kitchen.

'You've led a long and good life,' said the fairy, 'so I've come to reward you and tell you that you can make three wishes. Ask for absolutely anything you like and with one wave of my magic wand, you can have it.'

The old lady found this very difficult to believe, so she asked the fairy to turn the teapot into lots of lovely money. The fairy waved her magic wand and the teapot promptly turned into a pile of money.

'My!' exclaimed the old lady. 'It really does work! Now, can you make me look young and beautiful?'

The fairy waved her wand again and in a few seconds the little old lady was transformed into someone looking young and beautiful.

'And now I'd like you to turn my dear old cat into a handsome young man.'

This, too, was soon done, and the fairy left the old-but-now-young-and-beautiful-looking-lady alone in her kitchen with the handsome young man who had formerly been a cat.

The lady turned to the man and sighed: 'At last! Now I want to make love to you for the rest of the day and night!'

The man looked at her, then said, in a very high pitched voice: 'Then you shouldn't have taken me to the vet's, should you?'

968. My girlfriend says there are things a girl shouldn't do before 20. I'm not too keen on an audience, either.

969. Man: 'What would I have to give you to get a little kiss?'

Girl: 'Chloroform.'

970. Pretty young girl: 'If I go up to your room do you promise to be good?'

Young man: 'Why – I promise to be FANTASTIC!'

971. His girlfriend is such a snob she won't eat hot dogs unless they've been registered at the Kennel Club.

972. It was at a fancy dress party and the young girl said to the man: 'I'm supposed to be a turkey – what are you?'

'Sage and onions,' he replied.

973. Simon: 'I know of only one way that a girl can remain a good girl on holiday in Greece.'

Hazel: 'And what way is that?'

Simon: 'I was right! I thought you wouldn't know.'

974. Her boyfriend only had one fault. He had Tarzan eyes – they swung from limb to limb.

975. Mavis fell in love with her boyfriend at second sight – the first time she didn't know he had any money.

976. George: 'Sir, I don't quite know how to ask this.'
Mr Smith: 'Ask what?'
George: 'Well, I'd like your daughter for my wife.'
Mr Smith: 'Don't be ridiculous! I know we live in liberated times, but I don't think I'd like my daughter to go off with your wife.'

977. Young man: 'Do you think you could be happy with a man like me?'
Young girl: 'Of course! So long as he wasn't *too* much like you.'

978. David saw a beautiful young girl walking along the beach, dressed in an extremely tight pair of denim shorts which emphasized every movement of her walk.
Being a daring sort, he went up to the girl and said: 'I'm sorry to trouble you – but I'm fascinated about your shorts. How can anyone possibly manage to get inside such a tight garment?'
The beautiful young girl smiled and replied: 'You can start by asking me out to dinner.'

979. Sally: 'I don't think I'll be able to do much work today. I'm so sleepy! I didn't manage to get to sleep until after three.'
Samantha: 'I'm not surprised you're tired! One man – or two at the most – are enough for me. But three . . . ?'

980. A man of thirty was talking to his girlfriend. 'I've been asked to get married hundreds of times,' he said.
'Oh!' replied his girlfriend, rather astonished. 'Who by?'
'My parents,' he answered.

981. The young couple had a beef stew romance – she was always beefing, and he was always stewed.

982. My girlfriend rejected me because she said she liked the little things in life – a little house in the country, a little yacht, a little multi-millionaire . . .

983. 'If I refuse to go to bed with you, will you *really* commit suicide?'
'That has been my usual procedure, yes.'

984. Mabel is the best housekeeper in the world. She's been divorced fifteen times – and she's still got the house.

985. 'Darling, I want to make love before we get married,' said the girl, snuggling up to her boyfriend.
'But it won't be long until July, dear,' he replied.
'Oh!' she exclaimed enthusiastically, 'and how long will it be then?'

986. Trying to persuade a baby to go to bed is hardest when she's beautiful and about eighteen years old.

987. 'Excuse me, madam, we are doing a survey. Can you tell me what you think of sex on the television?'
'Very uncomfortable.'

988. Passenger: 'I lost my virginity on this bus.'
Friend: 'Why didn't you ask at the depot if anyone had handed it in?'

989. She started licking my cheek tenderly. I said: 'Do you love me?'
She said: 'No – but I need the salt.'

990. Rodney: 'Who was the blonde I saw you with last night?'
John: 'That was the dark-haired girl you saw me with on Monday.'

991. 'Did he have a great weakness for ladies?'
'No – a great strength!'

992. Dennis knew he was really getting places with his girlfriend, Carol, when she invited him around to her parents' house, saying: 'We can have a great time together, I'm sure, as my parents are going to a concert and will be out the whole evening.'

Thus, on the great day he stopped in at a chemist's shop on his way to his girlfriend's house. The chemist was such a friendly man that Dennis found himself confiding to him about how beautiful Carol was and how he hoped she would appreciate his thoughtfulness in coming prepared with some contraceptives.

When Dennis arrived at Carol's house he found her waiting for her father to come home from work, while Carol's mother was getting ready for the concert.

As soon as Carol's father arrived home, Dennis suddenly became very agitated and kept stammering and suggested, loudly: 'C . . . Carol, I . . . I . . . th . . . think we should j . . . join your p . . . parents and go to the c . . . c . . . concert tonight.'

'Oh!' said Carol, disappointedly. 'I didn't know you like classical music, Dennis.'

'I don't,' he hissed. 'But then, I didn't know your father was a chemist!'

993. My sister had to give up her last boyfriend because he was tall, dark, and hands . . .

994. 'Will you marry me?' asked the young man, getting down on his knees and offering the girl a glittering ring.

'Ooooh!' exclaimed the girl, 'are they real diamonds?'

'I hope so,' said the man. 'Because if they aren't I've been swindled out of ten pounds.'

995. Richard had been ship-wrecked on a desert island for the last three years with only the company of his faithful dog and a pig that had roamed into his encampment.

Now three years is a long time for a man to be without female company so, as night times approached, Richard's eyes were attracted more and more towards the pig. Then one night, when he thought the dog was fast asleep, he stealthily crawled in the pig's direction. All at once the dog awoke and gave a jealous growl and, gripping Richard by the pants, pulled him back to his bed roll.

As other evenings passed by and the inclination grew stronger, Richard tried to sneak his way across the encampment but each time that he attempted to move in that direction he was met with a growl from the jealous dog.

One day his luck broke as he walked along the beach for he discovered a scantily dressed young woman lying unconscious upon the sand, obviously the victim of a sunken vessel. He decided to leave her where she lay until she gained consciousness but covered her with palm leaves to retain heat.

After an hour she stirred, wriggled her bronzed young figure and opening her lovely wide blue eyes, she noticed Richard.

'You saved me, didn't you?' she asked, now standing upright. He nodded.

'To show my appreciation you can have anything you wish,' she said, shyly.

'I can? Wow!' Richard was delighted and thumped the air with his fist.

'What do you want?' said the shy beautiful girl.

Richard again yelled, the sound deafening out the breaking waves. His mouth opened as his imagination worked overtime. 'Will you take the dog for a walk?' he asked.

996. Although she was only the architect's daughter, she let the borough surveyor.

997. It's hard to keep a good girl down – but lots of fun trying.

998. Martin: 'What do virgins eat for breakfast?'
Emma: 'I don't know.'
Martin: 'Huh! Just as I thought!'

999. My girlfriend says she is 'pushing thirty' – but slapped my face when I asked her from which direction.

1000. I'm going to stop my wife nagging me. I'm going to de-voice her!

1001. Two young girls were talking in the office canteen when the subject, as usual, came round to discussing the men in their office.
'I wouldn't have anything to do with Graham Smith, if I were you,' said one of the girls.
'But why not?' asked her friend. 'He seems such a nice sort of man.'
'Ah! But he knows an awful lot of very dirty songs.'
'But surely he doesn't sing them in the office?' asked the friend. 'I've never heard him singing dirty songs.'
'No, perhaps not – but he certainly whistles them!'

1002. When I met my boyfriend we were both rough and ready. He was rough – I was ready.

1003. The mother of one of the servants came storming into the lord's manor, demanding to see the lord.
'What is it you want?' asked the lord, when the angry woman was brought before him.
'It's about my daughter, Jenny – she works here,' said the woman. 'You've got her pregnant!'
'Don't worry,' replied the lord. 'If she really *is*

pregnant then I'll give you some money – and when the little one comes along I'll set up a trust with at least half a million. Does that seem fair?'

'You're very kind,' agreed the woman, 'but if it doesn't happen – will you give her another chance?'

1004. He used to go out with a girl called Ruth. Then she left him, so he became ruthless.

1005. The man kissed the girl passionately.
  Girl: 'I thought a quick one before dinner meant a drink.'

1006. 'He loves you terribly.'
  'I keep telling *him* that.'

1007. There's nothing like a mink coat to thaw a cold shoulder.

1008. A ventriloquist on tour was looking desperately for digs when someone suggested that he drive down the country lane to a lonely farm. 'There's a farmer down there living on his own who occasionally takes in lodgers,' he was told. Sure enough, the farmer welcomed him with open arms since, as he lived on his own, he was glad of the company.
  After devouring a more than ample evening meal the farmer asked if he would like to view the farm. Of course the ventriloquist agreed and strode out into the evening air.
  The farmer directed him immediately to the stables and it was plain to see that they were his pride and joy. Opening the first stable door they peered in and the noise disturbed a donkey that turned to stare at its visitors. Not telling the farmer that he was a ventriloquist, he decided to have a leg pull at the farmer's expense.
  'Does the farmer treat you well?' asked the ventriloquist.

'Oh, yes,' came the reply that seemed to come from the donkey. 'He gives me carrots regularly.'

The farmer's eyes seemed to bulge. 'Do you know something?' he told the ventriloquist. 'I've had that donkey for fifteen years and it's never spoken to me once!'

Still amazed, the farmer unlocked the second door and a cow turned its head. The ventriloquist threw his voice.

'And what do you want?' said the cow. 'I've already been milked. Now moo-ve off and let me get some rest.'

The door was closed on the cow by a bemused farmer as he missed the next door and directed his visitor to the one further along.

'What's in here?' the visitor asked, turning back.

'Don't go in there,' the farmer demanded and started breaking into a sweat. 'I've got a prize stallion in this one.'

The curiosity of the ventriloquist became aroused and his insistence on the farmer opening the door became an obsession.

'All right, all right,' said the agitated farmer, searching for the key. 'But if the pig in there says I made love to it last night – it's a LIAR!'

1009. The young girl arrived home late from an evening out with her boyfriend. As she stomped into her flat and slammed the door her flatmate came out of her bedroom to see what all the noise was about.

'Oh!' exclaimed the girl. 'Bill really is the limit! I had to slap his face several times this evening!'

'Why, what did he do?' asked her flatmate, eagerly.

'Nothing, unfortunately,' muttered the pretty young girl. 'I had to slap his face to see if he was awake.'

1010. Man was made before woman to give him time to think of an answer to her first question.

SCHOOL

1011. A small boy came home after his first day at a new school and said to his mother: 'The teacher asked me if I had any brothers and sisters who might be coming to school.'

'That's nice of her to take such an interest in us. Did you say that you were an only child?' replied the mother.

'Yes,' the boy replied. 'And all she said was: "thank goodness".'

1012. A little girl had just started to go to school, and of course, her mother was interested and wanted to know all about it.

'Does your teacher call out your names in the morning?' she asked. The little girl shook her head.

'Then how does she know if all the boys and girls are there?' said her mother.

'Well,' said her little daughter, 'the first thing we do when we go into the classroom is to say the Lord's Prayer. Then at the end of it, we all say "I'm in".'

1013. Little Albert came home from school one day with tears streaming down his cheeks.

'What on earth's the matter Albert?' asked his mother.

'They keep laughing at me in the school yard and calling me "werewolf" mother.'

His mother comforted him and told him how children tend to be cruel at times.

'But do I look like a werewolf mother?'

'Of course not, Albert. Now wipe away all those tears then go upstairs and comb your face!'

1014. 'Mummy,' said little Desmond, 'at school today the religious teacher kept going on about "dust to dust and ashes to ashes". What did she mean?'

'I expect it means that we all come from dust and that, in the end, we'll return to dust.'

That evening, Desmond came running down the stairs from his room, calling anxiously for his mother.

'What is it? What's the matter?' she asked.

'Mummy! Come up quickly and look under my bed. Either someone has gone or someone is just coming!'

1015. A boy, whose father had received a bad school report of his son asked: 'What do you think the trouble with me is, Dad – heredity or environment?'

1016. 'Now,' said the lecturer, 'I shall be talking today about the heart, lungs, liver . . .'

'Oh, dear,' murmured one of the students, 'I just can't stand organ recitals.'

1017. A teacher asked her class of small children to make a crayon picture of the Old Testament story which they liked best.

One small boy depicted a man driving an old car. In the back seat were two passengers, both scantily dressed.

'It's a nice picture,' said the teacher, 'but what story does it tell?'

The young artist seemed surprised at the question. 'Well,' he exclaimed, 'doesn't it say in the Bible that God drove Adam and Eve out of the Garden of Eden?'

1018. A teacher warned her pupils to wrap up warm against the cold winter, and to show how important this was she told them of the true story of her little brother

208

who took his sledge out in the snow one day. Unfortunately, her brother hadn't been wrapped up properly and he caught pneumonia and died a few days later.

There was silence in the classroom for a few moments, then a small voice at the back said: 'Please Miss, what happened to his sledge?'

1019. A little girl was trying to persuade her father to come to the school Nativity Play. 'I'm to be one of the Three Kings,' she said, 'and carry the Frankenstein.'

1020. A teacher, when she entered the classroom, noticed a pool of water near the blackboard. 'Who is responsible for this?' she asked.

There was no reply, so she said: 'Now, I want whoever did this to own up. So we will all close our eyes and then the guilty boy must come forward and write his name on the blackboard.'

All closed their eyes and presently there were furtive footsteps up to the blackboard, a little pause and then the scratching of chalk on the board followed by the retreating footsteps of the writer.

When the command was given for all to open their eyes, it was seen that there was another little pool of water, while on the blackboard was written: 'The phantom piddler strikes again.'

1021. My son got expelled from a computer course. He kept putting Tipp-ex on the screen.

1022. Religious knowledge teacher: 'Now, Timothy, where do naughty boys and girls go?'

Timothy: 'Behind the bicycle shed in the playground.'

1023. A boy said to his mother: 'I want to be early at school this afternoon so that I can sit in the front seat. We're going to have a lesson on sex.'

When he returned later in the day she asked him if the lesson had interested him as he seemed somewhat disappointed.

'Pooh!' he replied. 'It was all theory.'

1024. 'What are you making, Tommy?' asked the woodwork teacher.

'A portable,' replied the small boy.

'A portable what?'

'I don't know yet, sir. I've only made the handle.'

1025. The class were having a lesson on religious instruction. At the end a boy put up his hand and said: 'Please, miss, I know where God lives.'

'Oh,' said the teacher, 'and where is that?'

'He lives at 159 High Street,' came the reply. 'I was passing there this morning,' went on the boy, 'and a woman who was knocking called out, "God, are you not up yet?"'

1026. A Sunday School teacher asked her young class: 'Can anyone tell me who Matthew was?' There was no reply.

'Does anyone know who Peter was?'

Then a small boy remarked: 'Please, miss, I fink he was a wabbit.'

1027. Yet another Sunday School teacher asked one of her pupils if he could say who it was that sat at God's right hand.

Little Jimmy paused, then hazarded a guess: 'Mrs God, do you think?'

1028. 'Hello,' said the school teacher, answering the phone. 'This is Miss Engels of Form Two.'

'Hello,' said the voice on the phone. 'I'm phoning to tell you that Jim Brown is sick and won't be coming to school today.'

'Oh, I *am* sorry to hear that,' commented the teacher. 'Who is that speaking?'

The voice on the telephone replied: 'This is my father.'

1029. A school teacher, thinking to test the intelligence of his class, asked to be given a number of two figures. '49' called out one boy and the teacher immediately wrote 94 on the blackboard.

'Another number?' he called again, and another boy said '97' and the teacher wrote 79.

At a third request a big gangling lad called out '66 – and now muck about with that one!'

1030. The two little girls were talking at school during playtime.

'Do you know how old teacher is?' asked Janice.

'No,' replied Sarah, 'but I know how to find out.'

'Oh. How?'

'Take off her knickers.'

'Take off her knickers!' exclaimed Janice. 'How will *that* tell us?'

'Well, in my knickers it says "4 to 6 years".'

1031. 'Now children,' said a Sunday School teacher, 'you have just heard the story of Jonah and the whale. Can you tell me what this story teaches?'

'Yes, miss,' said one boy. 'It teaches that you can't keep a good man down.'

1032. Little Simon was the school swot – the other kids used to pick him up and bash flies with him.

1033. A kindergarten school teacher smiled pleasantly at a man who was seated opposite to her in a bus, but he did not respond. Suddenly, she realized her mistake and said aloud: 'Oh, do excuse me, but I thought for a moment that you were the father of one of my children.' She hurriedly got off the bus at the next stop.

1034. Small boy: 'Please, miss, would you be angry and tell me off for something I didn't do?'

Teacher: 'No, of course not.'

Small boy: 'Oh, good! Then I can tell you I haven't done my homework.'

1035. Mother: 'Where did you get that black eye, Jimmy? Didn't I tell you that good little boys never fight?'

Jimmy: 'Yes, mother, and I believed you. I thought he was a good little boy and I hit him, and then I found out he wasn't.'

1036. Mother: 'Now, let's see how clever you are, Katie. If I have six sweets and someone gives me another two sweets, how many sweets do I have?'

Very young daughter: 'I don't know, mummy. At nursery school we do all our sums with fingers or apples.'

1037. Teacher: 'Susan, give me a sentence beginning with "I".'

Susan: 'I is . . .'

Teacher (angrily): 'Susan! How many more times do I have to tell you! You must *always* say "I am"!'

Susan: 'All right, miss. I am the letter in the alphabet after H.'

1038. A small boy, absent from school for two days, returns.

'Hello, Barry,' said his teacher. 'Why have you been away from school?'

'Sorry, miss, my dad got burnt.'

'Oh!' said the teacher, 'nothing serious, I hope.'

'They don't mess about at the Crematorium, miss!'

212

1039. Lecturer to rowdy audience: 'I will not begin until this room settles down.'

Student: 'Go home and sleep it off!'

1040. Woman: 'Tell me, Des, how do you like school?'

Des: 'Closed.'

1041. Teacher: 'You've put your shoes on the wrong feet.'

Small boy: 'But these are the only feet I've got.'

1042. Teacher: 'What is the difference between the death rate in Victorian England and the present day?'

Pupil: 'It's the same, sir. One per person.'

1043. A teacher was checking her children's knowledge of proverbs. 'Cleanliness is next to what?' she asked.

'Impossible!' a small boy replied with great feeling.

1044. Claude's teacher said his handwriting was so bad the only profession he could follow on leaving school was to be a doctor.

1045. Teacher: 'Where are you from?'

New pupil: 'Devon, miss.'

Teacher: 'Which part?'

New pupil: 'All of me, miss.'

1046. The Sunday School teacher was talking to her class of ten-year-olds when she suddenly asked: 'Now, why do you think the Children of Israel made a Golden Calf?'

The children were silent until one spotty little boy put up his hand and said: 'Please, miss, perhaps it was because they didn't have enough gold to make a cow.'

1047. Teacher: 'If I were to ask you to add 9,731 to

237 and then halve it, what do you think you would get?'

Simon: 'The wrong answer, sir.'

1048. Pupil: 'Can I have a cigarette?'

Teacher: 'Good heavens! No, certainly not! Do you want to get me into trouble?'

Pupil: 'Well, all right then, miss. But I'd rather have a cigarette.'

1049. A school teacher asked the class, 'Who wrote *"Hamlet"*?' and one boy replied: 'Please sir, it wasn't me.'

The teacher was mentioning this that same evening in the local and the story provoked much laughter, especially from one man who, after wiping his eyes, blurted out: 'And I expect the little beggar wrote it all the time.'

1050. Young Alfie was forever turning up late for school but as the lad was the son of a farmer and obviously farm jobs were shared between the family, the teacher made allowances for the lad.

That was until one morning when Alfie slipped into the classroom very late indeed.

'Now then, now then,' shouted Miss Barlow in the most threatening voice she could muster.

'I'm very sorry, miss,' answered a nervous Alfie, beginning to shake, 'but I had my farm duties to see to, miss.'

'And farm duties are more important than school?' Miss Barlow closed in on the crouching Alfie. 'And what did this duty entail?'

'I had to take the bull down to the cow, miss,' explained Alfie.

'And . . .' Miss Barlow slammed her ruler onto the desk. 'Couldn't your father have done that?'

'Oh no, miss,' explained Alfie. 'It has to be the bull!'

1051. A father asked the headmaster for help, informing him that his son had got the gambling habit and that he was anxious for the boy to grow out of it. 'I'll see what I can do,' replied the headmaster.

When the father called for his boy at the end of the term the headmaster said: 'I think that I've cured your son of the gambling habit. I'll tell you what happened. One day I saw that he was looking at my beard and he said, "Sir, is that a real beard or is it a false one? I wouldn't mind betting five pounds that it is false." "All right," I replied, "I'll take your bet. Now pull it and see." Of course I made the boy pay me the five pounds, so I think I've cured him all right.'

'Oh, dear,' groaned the father. 'He bet me ten pounds that he would pull your beard before the term ended!'

1052. Teacher: 'Now, James, if you bought fifty doughnuts for one pound, what would each one be?'

James: 'Stale, miss! They'd have to be, at that price.'

1053. Sunday School teacher: 'Now, Jonathan, can you tell me what sort of people go to Heaven?'

Jonathan: 'Dead ones, miss.'

1054. A boy was asked in an examination paper to state what an atoll and a cyclone were and whether they were natural phenomena or scientific discoveries. With delightful simplicity he answered: 'God made them both.'

1055. Teacher: 'Tell me, Amber, is the world flat or is it round?'

Amber: 'Neither, miss. My mum keeps telling me it's crooked.'

1056. Chemistry teacher: 'What can you tell me about nitrates?'

215

Pupil: 'Well, sir . . . er . . . they're a lot dearer than day rates.'

1057. Little Fred came home from school after a particularly hard day and said to his mother: 'I wish I'd lived in olden days.'

'Why?' asked his mother, curious to know the reason.

'Because then I wouldn't have so much history to learn.'

1058. Teacher: 'Everything you do is wrong. How can you expect to get a job when you leave school if everything you do is inaccurate?'

Pupil: 'Well, sir! I'm going to be a TV weatherman.'

1059. Religious knowledge teacher: 'Now, children, I've just described all the pleasures of Heaven. Hands up all those who want to go there?'

All the children put their hands up, except for Debbie.

Religious knowledge teacher: 'Debbie, why don't you want to go to Heaven?'

Debbie (tearfully): 'I'd like to go, miss, but me mum said I had to come straight home after school.'

1060. Another Sunday School class had just been hearing about the parable of the prodigal son. 'Now,' said the Sunday School teacher, 'who was not glad to know of the prodigal's return?'

'Please, sir,' replied one boy, 'the fatted calf.'

1061. An Irish schoolmaster offered a reward to any boy who could tell him who was the greatest man in history.

'Christopher Columbus,' said one boy.

'George Washington,' answered another.

'St Patrick,' shouted out a little Jewish boy.

'The prize is yours,' said the schoolmaster. 'But, tell me, how came you to think of St Patrick?'

'Well, right down in my heart, I knew it was Moses,' replied the boy, 'but business is business.'

1062. A new and rather young lady teacher had joined the school and one day she found written on the blackboard the words: 'Johnny Jones can kiss and cuddle better than any boy in the class.'

'Who wrote this?' she demanded, and after a while she found that Johnny Jones had written it himself. 'Right,' she said, 'you can stay behind after class.'

When he eventually appeared, several of the other boys clustered round him and said: 'What happened, Johnny? Did she cane you?'

'Oh, no, nothing like that,' replied Johnny, who was rather a big boy for his age, 'but it pays to advertise.'

1063. The University lecturer was speaking to an audience of townspeople. He was attempting to prove there was a definite connection between happiness and the amount of sex in people's lives.

To help prove his point, he asked those in the audience who indulged every night to raise their right hands. Only five per cent did so, all laughing merrily.

He then asked how many indulged about once per week, and seventy per cent raised their hands, smiling contentedly as they did so.

Then the people who indulged once every month were asked to raise their hands, but it was noticeable that these people neither laughed nor smiled.

The lecturer felt that he had proved his point – but to show how obvious the matter was, he asked those who only indulged once every year to raise their hands. A tall man at the back of the hall leapt from his chair, waving his hand and laughing loudly.

The lecturer was astonished at this apparent contradiction to his lecture, and he asked the man if he could explain why he was so happy.

The man replied: 'Certainly. It's tonight! It's tonight!'

SHOPS & SERVICES

1064. An elderly shopkeeper was ill and his family, who thought he was dying, had gathered around his bedside. Suddenly the old man roused up and said: 'Is Rachel here?'

'Yes, I am here,' said his wife.

'Is John here?' went on the old man.

'Yes, I am here,' said his son.

'Is Sarah here?' he again asked.

'Yes, I am here,' said his daughter.

The old man sat bolt upright in bed and yelled: 'Then who the hell is looking after the shop?'

1065. 'This pair of shoes you sold me last week is ridiculous! One of them has a heel at least two inches shorter than the other. What do you expect me to do?'

'Limp.'

1066. Customer: 'I'd like to buy a novel, please.'

Bookshop assistant: 'Certainly, madam. Do you have the title or name of the author?'

Customer: 'Not really. I was hoping you could suggest something suitable that I could read.'

Bookshop assistant: 'No problem. Do you like light or heavy reading?'

Customer: 'It doesn't matter. I've left the car just outside the shop.'

1067. The lift in the large hotel was extremely crowded, and as the lift attendant closed the doors he called: 'Which floors, please?'

A young man standing near the back of the lift cried out: 'Ballroom!'

'Oh, I'm sorry,' said the large lady in front of him. 'I didn't know I was crushing you that much.'

1068. A man bought a bath and was leaving the shop with his purchase when the shop assistant called: 'Do you want a plug?'

'Why?' asked the man. 'Is it electric?'

1069. In the High Street there were three shops, all in the same line of business and standing next to one another. Seeking to improve trade, the one on the left put up a notice: 'Old Established – only goods of quality.'

The one on the right countered with: 'Newly Established – no old goods sold.'

The middle shop merely erected a sign stating: 'Main Entrance.'

1070. A woman went into a shop to buy a chicken. The shopkeeper produced one but the woman said: 'Have you one a little larger?'

'Just a moment,' said the shopkeeper and he went into an inner room and generally plumped up the bird. Actually it was the only one he had.

'There,' he said, reappearing. 'How's that?'

'Oh, that's much better,' the woman replied. 'Now, I'll take both!'

1071. Have you heard the story of the grocer who backed onto the bacon slicer when it was in action? Now his customers are getting a little behind with their orders.

1072. Then there was the grocer who advertised for a boy 'to be partly indoors and partly outdoors'.

One applicant asked: 'What becomes of me when the door closes?'

1073. I went into a bakery. I said: 'How much for these two pies?'

The girl behind the counter said: '90 pence.'

I said: 'How much is it for one?'

She said: '60 pence.'

I said: 'I'll have the other one.'

1074. Two shopkeepers were talking. The first one asked: 'How do you find business these days?'

The other replied: 'Terrible. Even the people who don't intend to pay have stopped ordering.'

1075. Customer: 'Please do you have a dress that would match the colour of my eyes?'

Honest salesgirl: 'I'm sorry, madam, but they don't make material in bloodshot.'

1076. A shopkeeper was held up by a man waving a bunch of flowers at him in a threatening manner. It was robbery with violets.

1077. Customer of large department store: 'Why do you look so depressed?'

Department store lift attendant: 'Because my job keeps bringing me down.'

1078. It was a quiet morning in the local general store and that was why Sammy the shop assistant stood with his hands on his hips gazing through the large window, watching people moving about along Market Street.

Amongst the old women and children scurrying along the street, Sammy's eye was sternly fixed on a huge hulking man propelling himself like a human ape along the street. 'I bet a fellow like that makes his money in a wrestling ring,' thought Sammy. A smile covered his face as a thought entered his head: 'I shouldn't like him to fall on me. Oh, no!'

The huge man crossed the road as another two customers entered the shop. Sammy moved behind the counter as the 'ting' of the doorbell told him that the man had entered the shop. Standing in front of Sammy his frame blotted out the light.

'I want half a loaf,' he said.

'I'm sorry, sir,' gulped Sammy, 'but we don't sell half a loaf. At least, we never have,' he gulped again. He looked up at the man's scarred face and decided to follow that with: 'But I'll ask the manager.'

Sammy quickly left the counter and entered a side door. 'You won't believe this,' Sammy told the manager. 'There's a chap just come in who must be seven feet tall, wider than a barn door, with a head bigger than the town hall clock and a face that would scare a police dog . . . and he's asked for half a loaf.'

Just at that moment something told him to turn around and when he did he found the man towering over him. All the blood drained from Sammy's face as the smile disappeared. 'And do you know something?' went on Sammy. 'This gentleman wants the other half!'

1079. Tailor: 'Your suit will be ready in six weeks, sir.'

Customer: 'Six weeks! But God made the whole world in only six days!'

Tailor: 'Quite true, sir. But look what state the world is in!'

1080. A professor of Greek tore his suit and took it to a tailor named Acidopulos, from Athens. Mr Acidopulos examined the suit and asked: 'Euripides?'

'Yes,' said the professor. 'Eumenides?'

1081. One old antique dealer called upon another. Said the first: 'I've got something to show you.' Then, taking a small box out of his pocket, he opened it and revealed a little piece of dark wood. 'Piece of the Ark,' he said.

The other made no reply, but going to a cabinet, he produced a similar box with an identical piece of wood.

Then the first dealer put his hand in his pocket again and took out another little box, this time containing a small piece of old lace. 'Piece of the Queen of Sheba's nightdress,' he said.

The second dealer again made no reply, but going to the cabinet again took out another box with a similar piece of lace.

Thereupon the first dealer, very mad, put his hand in his pocket and produced a small round black object. Glaring at the other, he said: 'King Nebuchadnezzar's left knee cap. And,' he went on, 'don't make out you've got t'other one, because I've got it at home!'

1082. Have you ever been to a clumsy barber? I was waiting in the barber's last week whilst he worked on a man sitting uncomfortably in the chair.

First he nicked his right ear with the razor and drew blood, then he cut the soft part under his nose before moving to the other side to cut into his other ear.

'Have you been here before?' the barber asked the now irate customer.

'No,' came the reply. 'I lost my arm in the war!'

1083. Claude (looking at his barber's bill): 'What? Ten pounds just to cut my hair – but I'm nearly bald . . .'

Barber: 'I know, sir. My charge is one pound for cutting the hair and nine pounds for search fees.'

1084. Barber: 'Were you wearing a red scarf when you came in?'

Customer: 'No.'
Barber: 'Oh! Then I must have cut your throat.'

1085. Barber: 'Sir, how would you like your hair cut?'
Customer: 'Off.'

1086. My brother came out of jail after 5 years and when he tried on his suit he found a laundry ticket in the top pocket. He took the ticket in and they told him his cleaning will be ready on Friday!

1087. Beach inspector: 'Why have you applied for the job of lifeguard? You're just wasting my time! You can't even swim!'
Job applicant: 'I know. But at seven feet two inches in height I can wade out quite a long way!'

1088. 'I knew you needed an optician,' said the optician to the young man.
'How did you know that?'
'Simple! You just walked in through the window.'

1089. The bossy, unattractive woman said to the photographer: 'Make sure your photos do me justice.'
'Madam,' replied the photographer, 'you don't want justice – you want mercy.'

1090. Our dustman got married last week. He carried the bride over the threshold and dropped half of her on the path.

1091. Mrs Smith: 'Why have you come today? You were supposed to repair the doorbell yesterday.'
Electrician: 'I did come yesterday, but after I rang three times and got no answer I thought you must be out.'

1092. To the sound of breaking glass, an estate agent told a couple who were visiting one of the houses on his books: 'We're only a stone's throw from the local school.'

1093. Estate agent to young house-hunting couple: 'First you tell me what you can afford. Then we'll have a good laugh about it and go from there.'

SHORTIES

1094. Owing to a strike at the meteorological office, there will be no weather tomorrow.

1095. I met Claudia Hott-Iron yesterday – she made a great impression on me.

1096. The only thing that prevents me from being a bigamist is the thought of having two mothers-in-law.

1097. Inscription on a nun's tombstone: 'Returned – unopened.'

1098. Women are to blame for all the lying men do – they will insist on continually asking questions.

1099. The main difference between men and boys is that men's toys cost more money.

1100. A carpet said to a floor today: 'OK, don't move. I've got you covered.'

1101. Not to mention the all-metal noticeboard which commented this morning: 'You can't pin anything on me.'

1102. I've always believed in love at first sight – ever since I looked into a mirror.

1103. 'I can't stop telling lies.'
  'I don't believe you!'

1104. Every Saturday and Sunday my father goes to the Old Folks Club. I don't know exactly what he does there – but he's got eight notches in his walking stick.

1105. A man tried to stab me early this evening. He was a man after my own heart.

1106. I used to be engaged to a contortionist – until she broke it off.

1107. Masochist: 'Hit me!'
  Sadist: 'No.'

1108. The only reason there is a population explosion is because it's such great fun to light the fuse.

1109. We call my friend Goliath because he keeps getting stoned.

1110. Three tonnes of human hair to be made into wigs was stolen today from East Grinstead. Police are combing the area.

1111. Jeffrey: 'We have a Red Indian toaster at home.'
  Jeremy: 'What's a Red Indian Toaster?'
  Jeffrey: 'Instead of the toast popping up it sends up smoke signals.'

1112. The hippie cannibal ate three square meals a day.

1113. A hymn has recently been dedicated to a Birmingham corset factory. It is 'All Is Safely Gathered In'.

1114. One cannibal wanted to become a detective so he could grill all his suspects.

1115. The largest women in the USA are Mrs Sippy and Miss Oory.

1116. Inscription on the tombstone of a hypochondriac: 'See – I *told* you I was ill.'

1117. I am told that it takes three sheep to make a sweater but I didn't know that they could knit!

1118. Interviewer: 'What are those tiny bongos dangling from your ears?'
Pop star: 'Oh, they're just my eardrums.'

1119. 'Why don't you answer the phone?'
'Because it's not ringing.'
'Why must you leave everything until the last minute?'

1120. A verbal contract isn't worth the paper it's written on.

1121. I went on a Chinese diet. They only give you one chopstick.

1122. Last week a man fell into a tank of beer and came to a bitter end.

1123. The two red corpuscles – they loved in vein.

1124. For sale: two single beds and a worn carpet.

1125. Claude was so wealthy that even the bags under his eyes had his initials on them.

1126. She shook hands with the faith healer and broke two fingers!

1127. We took him to hospital because he swallowed a spoon. He never stirred all day.

1128. People who cough loudly never go to the doctor – they go to the cinema.

1129. Where there's a will, there are relatives.

1130. If it wasn't for venetian blinds it would be curtains for all of us.

1131. It has recently been discovered that Wales is sinking into the sea – due to the many leeks in the ground.

1132. If at first you don't succeed you're just like 99.99% of the population.

1133. It has been said that strip poker is the only card game in which the more you lose, the more you have to show for it.

1134. He was thrown out of the Serious Crime Squad for laughing.

1135. The best distance between two points is cleavage.

1136. I've believed in reincarnation ever since I was a young frog.

1137. When asked for a donation to the local orphanage a man sent two orphans.

1138. Laugh and the world laughs with you: weep and you sleep alone.

1139. 'Whatever I say goes.'
'Please talk to yourself.'

1140. Uri Geller was washing his neck and his head fell off.

1141. At his show a little old lady on the front row threw her rent book on stage and said: 'Straighten that out!'

1142. The only thing you can be sure of getting on your birthday is a year older.

1143. 'I don't know what to do with my hands while I'm talking.'
'Why don't you hold them over your mouth?'

1144. A hypochondriac's life is a bed of neuroses.

1145. 'Get my broker.'
'Which one – stock or pawn?'

1146. Never try to make love in a field of corn. It goes against the grain.

1147. 'By the time we've paid for all the furniture we've just bought we shall be the proud owners of genuine antiques.'

1148. People who sleep like babies never have any.

1149. 'I'm an atheist – thank God!'

1150. Never tell a psychiatrist you're schizophrenic. He'll charge you double.

1151. One of the first signs of getting old is when your head makes dates your body can't keep.

1152. Success doesn't always go to the head – more often it goes to the mouth.

1153. Absence makes the heart go wander.

1154. The less people know, the more stubbornly they know it.

1155. Anyone who boasts about his ancestors is admitting that his family is better dead than alive.

SPEECHES & SPEAKING

1156. Advice to after dinner speakers: If after ten minutes you don't strike oil, then stop boring.

1157. In the days of the persecution of the early Christians, a party of these were led out into the arena to be fed to the lions. To the surprise of the emperor and his friends, as one of the lions came bounding out one of the Christians went up to it and whispered something in its ear, and the lion slunk away. This happened a second and yet a third time, whereupon the emperor stopped the proceedings and calling the Christian over said: 'If you will tell me what you said to make the lions stop from killing and eating you, then I will spare your life.'

The Christian replied: 'I merely remarked, "After dinner you will be required to say a few words."'

1158. 'Why did you walk out in the middle of my speech?' demanded the company Chairman of one of his senior executives. 'It was a very important meeting of shareholders and you chose the most crucial moment to walk out when I had been speaking for only forty-five minutes.'

'I'm sorry, sir,' replied the senior executive, 'but it wasn't anything personal. I was just sleepwalking.'

1159. A certain literary society had advertised a talk on Keats and at rather the last moment had asked the mayor, a well-meaning but ignorant man, to take the chair. After a few normal remarks on the occasion he concluded by saying: 'Now, I'm sure you're all as anxious as I am for the speaker to begin and let us know, just exactly, what are Keats?'

1160. A business executive had to make a speech at an important meeting attended by his business associates. He couldn't think of anything interesting to talk about, so in the end he decided to talk about sex.

When he arrived home his wife asked him how his speech had gone. He replied that it had been a huge success.

'But what did you talk about?'

The man thought for a few seconds, then replied: 'Oh, sailing.'

The following week one of the man's business colleagues approached the man's wife at a cocktail party and commented: 'That was a marvellous speech your husband made last week.'

'I know,' replied the wife. 'It's amazing. He's only tried it twice. The first time his hat blew off and the second time he was sea-sick.'

1161. At an embassy luncheon a young Englishman found himself seated next to a Chinaman. Wishing to be friendly, after soup had been served, he turned to the Chinaman and said: 'Likee soupee?' The Chinaman merely smiled and the Englishman thought: 'Poor chap, probably doesn't understand English.'

At the conclusion of the meal there were some speeches and to the Englishman's horror the Chinaman rose to respond to the toast of 'The Visitors' and in a discourse full of wit and epigram he made an excellent speech in perfect English.

As he sat down to applause, he turned to the Englishman and said: 'Likee speechee?'

1162. A speaker in Hyde Park was carrying on loudly against the tobacco habit. 'Yes, you,' he shouted to a small mixed audience, 'you dash into a tobacconist's, you put down your money and get a packet of cigarettes. But that is not the end of it, for in their wake follow beer, whisky, brandy and other intoxicants.'

'Blimey, guv'nor!' said a burly navvy. 'You might tell us the name of your tobacconist!'

SPORTS & GAMES

1163. The teacher asked a class to write a brief account of a cricket match. Soon all the children were very engrossed except for one boy who finished his essay in record time. When the teacher saw it, he understood. It read: 'Rain stopped play.'

1164. 'I have learnt some of white man's magic,' said

the African Chief on returning to his country after a brief stay in England.

'What?' asked his brother.

'First, you must make a smooth piece of ground and get grass to grow on it. Then you carefully tend the grass. After that you place some sticks in the grass and get some men to put on all-white clothes. Two of the men have to carry pieces of wood called "bats" and another man has to carry a red ball. After a bit of running about between the sticks by two of the men and some throwing of the red ball, it will rain.'

1165. A man walked into a fishmonger's, and asked to buy six trout. 'Certainly sir,' said the fishmonger, selecting the trout. He was about to wrap them up when the man said: 'No! Please don't wrap them up yet. Can you just gently throw them to me one by one?'

'I can,' replied the fishmonger. 'But why?'

'Well,' responded the man. 'I've been fishing all night and haven't caught anything. At least if you throw those trout to me and I catch them I can honestly say when I get home that I've caught six trout.'

1166. 1st fisherman: 'Is this a good river for fish?'

2nd fisherman: 'Yes. It's so good that none of them were willing to leave it.'

1167. Fred: 'The fishing today wasn't very good.'

Claude: 'But I thought you'd had fifty bites?'

Fred: 'So I did: one small fish and forty-nine mosquitoes.'

1168. 'I'm never taking my sister fishing again!' sighed the small boy to his mother.

'Why not?' asked his mother. 'I know she's only two but the water isn't very deep and you can swim, so what's the problem?'

'She keeps eating all my maggots and worms.'

1169. A footballer died and arrived at the gates of heaven where an angel awaited him. 'Now,' said the angel, 'before you enter here, is there anything that happened to you on earth upon which you would like your mind set at rest?'

The footballer thought for a moment and then said: 'There is one matter. I belonged to the famous St Mirren Club and one cup final when we were playing the Rangers, I scored a goal which I am sure was offside. It won us the match and the cup, but I've always been troubled about it.'

'Oh,' replied the angel, 'we know all about the goal up here. It was perfectly right, so you can banish all your doubts.'

'Oh, thank you, St Peter,' said the footballer.

The angel replied: 'But I'm not St Peter, you know.'

'Then who are you?' asked the footballer.

'St Mirren,' came the reply.

1170. My son has the making of a football hooligan: he threw a bottle at the referee yesterday. I wouldn't mind, but he broke the screen.

1171. The compulsive gambler at the roulette table was having a particularly bad run of luck when suddenly he heard a soft, ghostly voice in his ear say: 'Number Seven'.

The gambler furtively looked behind him, but there was no one near him who could possibly have made such a ghostly whisper. The gambler decided he had nothing to lose by backing the advice of the mysterious whisperer.

The number came up – number seven had won the gambler a small sum of money – but not enough to cover his earlier losses, so the gambler continued at the table. Again, the ghostly voice whispered: 'Number Seven', and the gambler followed the advice and won yet again.

This went on for some considerable time. Just before the gambler placed each bet the ghostly voice would whisper 'Number Seven', and the number seven always came up.

After this had happened nine times in succession, the gambler had collected quite a number of interested spectators – as well as winning well over five thousand pounds.

Then the ghostly voice whispered: 'Put everything on Number Five.' The gambler was surprised at the change in directions, but he decided to continue to follow the advice given him by the strange, ghostly voice.

The roulette wheel spun round, the gambler held his breath, the crowd around the table watched with astonishment – and the ball landed in number seven. And the ghostly voice in the gambler's ear said: 'Damn!'

1172. Fred had been a member of the British Legion Club ever since the war ended and such a club depended heavily on the money spent over the bar or by any other means. Now Fred was known throughout the club for his meanness and if a fiver passed from his pocket during the whole week into the club's till, then that must have been an occasion.

Such was the state of funds that a super raffle had been organized with the first prize of a new car for a contribution of just £5. Fred had been asked a few times if he wanted to enter the raffle but the organizer knew that £5 to him was the whole sum for the week.

'It's your last chance to enter,' the organizer pushed the book of tickets underneath Fred's nose, but all he did was shrug his shoulders and make his way into the snooker room.

Sitting himself down, Fred lazily thumbed through a newspaper that someone had left and thought to himself how the young members of society were attracted to the club. Young people of both sexes.

To give his eyes a rest he gazed towards the snooker table where a young lass was playing the game with her boyfriend. Fred's eyes nearly popped when he saw her bend over the table to play the ball, for whether by accident or design she was wearing no knickers and tatooed on each buttock was a number 6.

'It's a sign,' thought Fred, who believed in such things, which set his mind thinking of what it could be connected with. 'The draw!' It hit him as some kind of premonition that those two numbers had been sent to him as the winning number of the club's draw.

Rising sharply, he raced into the concert room where he found the organizer and asked if number 66 had been sold. Luckily it hadn't and Fred made the purchase.

The following evening was full of excitement for Fred as he opened the club door for he knew that the draw would have been already made. He made a beeline for the organizer and asked if the car had been claimed.

'No,' said the organizer.

'Did it have a six in it?' Fred wanted to know.

'As a matter of fact, it did.'

Fred's pulses raced as he searched for his ticket.

'Was it number 66?' he asked.

'Nearly,' said his friend, shrugging his shoulders and giving a consoling smile.

Fred tore up his ticket and placed it in an ashtray.

'What did win it?' asked Fred.

'606,' the organizer told him.

1173. In the days before betting shops came into existence, an old lady saw someone she thought was a poor man standing at a street corner. Being of a kindly disposition, she went up to him very quietly and, putting a five pound note into his hand, whispered: 'Charity, my man, charity.'

The next day she happened to pass that way again and to her surprise she saw the same man, who recognized her, and going up to her put a bundle of money into her hand, with the remark: 'You were lucky, lady. It came in at thirty-three to one.'

1174. A short tempered golfer had spent some time searching for a lost ball. Just as he was about to give up in disgust an elderly lady seated on the links nearby called out to him: 'Excuse me, but will I be breaking the rules if I tell you where it is?'

1175. After his last shot, Mr Smith turned to his caddie and asked: 'What do you think of my game?'

The caddie thought for a moment and then replied: 'I think your game is quite good, but I still prefer golf myself.'

1176. Golfer (very keen to improve his game): 'Do you notice any improvement in me today, caddie?'

Caddie: 'Yes, sir. You've had a haircut.'

1177. A woman player was asked by a friend: 'Do you like this course?'

'Well,' she replied, 'I can't really say. While I play regularly once a week, it always gets dark before I can complete the eighteen holes.'

1178. My wife claims that her golf is improving because today she hit the ball in one.

1179. Man: 'My doctor has advised me to give up golf.'

Friend: 'Why? Did he examine your heart?'

Man: 'No. He had a look at my score card.'

1180. A man was having a round of golf and said to his caddie: 'That chap who is just ahead of us, is he a new member? I don't remember seeing him before.'

The caddie replied: 'Yes, he is a new member. He

swore himself in yesterday.'

1181. Bill walked into his place of work wearing a heavy head bandage and knew that he'd have some explaining to do about his accident when confronted by the boss.

'I got it playing golf,' he explained.

'My word . . . it must have been some size of golf ball that hit you to make that sort of a mess!'

'It wasn't a golf ball that did it, it was a club,' he explained further.

'Sit down,' said the boss. 'This sounds interesting.'

Bill sat down gingerly, trying not to make any unnecessary movement with his head and the story began to unfold.

'I was playing a round of golf with my friend,' he went on, 'when my ball veered from the direction I had hit it and ended up in an adjoining field where cows were grazing. When I got there a lady golfer from another group was also busy looking for her lost ball. I found mine without any trouble, then I noticed that one of the cows kept giving a violent twitch of its tail. Lifting the tail I noticed a golf ball stuck in the cleavage beneath the cow's tail. Giving a whistle and a shout I beckoned the lady across. She looked puzzled at first, and then I raised the cow's tail. "This looks like yours," I said. It was then that she walloped me with her golf club.'

1182. Andrew came rushing into the clubhouse in a state of great agitation. 'I've just sliced the ball into a tree but it re-bounded and went into the road where it hit the rider of a motorbike who fell off his bike and then a lorry ran into him, causing its load of onions to spill all over the road which has caused more cars to crash and there are bodies and smashed vehicles all over the place. What can I do?'

The Club President thought deeply for a moment and

then suggested: 'Take it a bit easier on the backswing in future.'

1183. A chap who was a veritable 'rabbit' turned up at the golf clubhouse one day and announced that he was the proud father of triplets. Of course, this led to drinks all round, and afterwards the members thought that it would be a good idea to mark the occasion by presenting him with a small cup, especially as he had never won any club trophy.

In due course the presentation was made and the astonished recipient stammered his thanks, adding: 'What I should like to know is, is it mine for keeps now, or do I have to win it three years running?'

1184. Spring had just been and gone and as Tom's wife had not completed the chore of spring cleaning due to her commitments as Lady Vice Captain at the local golf club, Tom found himself with a pinafore around his waist and feather duster in hand, helping out.

He had changed the curtains downstairs and now here he was dusting in every nook and cranny in the bedroom. Standing on a chair, he raised himself above the level of the wardrobe and discovered a cardboard shoebox hidden at the back. 'Strange,' he thought as he pulled the box nearer to him then brought it down to rest on his wife's dressing table. Opening the box he discovered that it contained seven golf balls and a large amount of money.

Just then a noise was heard downstairs like the sound of an over-balanced golf bag hitting the hall floor then the closing of the front door. The happy sound of Emily, his wife, echoed through the house and he could tell that she had had a good day. 'I'm here, sweetheart,' shouted Tom and soon the bedroom door swung open.

Emily gave Tom a kiss then, when she saw the shoebox on the dressing table, she froze with astonishment. 'You found it then,' she whimpered timidly.

'What is going on?' demanded Tom, lifting up the golf balls.

'You see,' Emily replied, 'every time that I have been unfaithful to you I place a golf ball into the shoebox.'

'Oh?' was all that Tom could muster, feeling a little relieved that she had only been unfaithful seven times in all of their twenty years of marriage. 'And what about all this money?' he asked, running his fingers through it.

'I can explain,' she told her shaken husband. 'You see. Every time I got twenty-five balls I exchanged them for £30!'

1185. 'Are you sure you're a qualified jockey? You're sitting the wrong way round.'

'How do you know which direction I'm going in?'

1186. One man said to another: 'What became of that horse you bought at the sale a week or two ago?'

'Oh!' replied the other, 'it died.'

'What did you do about it?' asked the first man.

'Well,' said the other, 'I thought that it might be difficult to try and sue the previous owner, so I raffled it at £1 a time.'

'But didn't anybody kick up a fuss?' went on the first man.

'Only the winner,' replied the second man, 'so I gave him his money back.'

1187. An elderly lady was visiting Cornwall, and St. Michael's Mount, the small island off the coast, near Penzance, was pointed out to her.

'So that's St. Michael's Mount!' she exclaimed. 'Why, I always thought it was a racehorse belonging to Marks & Spencer!'

1188. 'Why is the horse trainer in hospital?'

'Well, he was boasting about how good he was – that he could train any four-legged creature to win any race and he'd even win riding it without a saddle. So someone gave him a porcupine . . .'

1189. The very expensive racehorse continually lost races which everyone had expected him to win.

'Perhaps what it needs is a bit more encouragement,' suggested the horse's owner.

So, just before the start of the next major race, the jockey warned the horse that if it lost this one it would be the end of its racing days and the horse would have to find work elsewhere – probably on a milk round in the country.

The horse nodded at the jockey to indicate that it understood the threat, and soon the race began.

Unfortunately, this horse was soon trailing behind all the others and as the jockey urged it forward with his whip the horse turned its head and said: 'Steady on, sir. I've got to be up early in the morning.'

1190. The racehorse owner had come down to the track to see for himself just how his horse was doing. The jockey had exercised it around the enclosure and after mounting, turned it to the direction of the starting post. The starting gates opened and the race began.

The horse was well placed at the start, but at the first jump someone in the crowd threw a bottle of whisky at them, causing the horse to lose some rhythm. The second time around and a Christmas stocking full of nuts came flying through the air in their direction, causing a loss of further yardage. The jockey was dreading passing that spot for the third time but as he did pass a Christmas pudding hit him with great force behind the neck.

The owner had been watching the performance of his horse and the jockey had some explaining to do. First he told him about the whisky bottle, then the nuts and finally the Christmas pudding being hurled in their direction.

'Dear me,' said the owner. 'It looks to me that you've been hampered!'

1191. Two men were climbing a particularly difficult mountain when one of them suddenly fell down a crevasse 500 feet deep.

'Are you all right, Bert?' called the man at the top of the crevasse.

'I'm still alive, thank goodness, Fred,' came the reply.

'Here, grab this rope,' said Fred, throwing a rope down to Bert.

'I can't grab it,' shouted Bert. 'My arms are broken.'

'Well, fit it around your legs.'

'I'm afraid I can't do that either,' apologised Bert. 'My legs are broken.'

'Put the rope in your mouth,' shouted Fred. So Bert put the rope in his mouth and Fred began to haul him to safety. 490 feet . . . 400 feet . . . 300 feet . . . 200 feet . . . 100 feet . . . 50 feet . . . and then Fred called: 'Are you all right, Bert?'

'Yeh-h-h . . . h . . . h . . .'

1192. 'So! Caught you at last,' hissed the game-keeper, emerging from the bushes behind a poacher.

'What do you mean?' asked the poacher.

'I saw you hastily throw that plucked bird back into the river as soon as you saw me. Look, there it is – still floating on the surface. And how do you explain all its feathers on your clothes?'

'Simple! The duck wanted to go for a swim so I'm minding its clothes.'

1193. Fred: 'I've just returned from a duck shoot.'
Tom: 'How was it?'

Fred: 'Terrible! All the others shot and I had to duck.'

1194. The epitaph seen on a snooker player's grave-stone: 'He's taken the long rest.'

1195. I've got nothing against watching professional wrestling – I just wish I had a low enough IQ to enjoy it.

1196. Gerald: 'I understand the sports and social club is looking for a treasurer.'
Edward: 'That's right.'
Gerald: 'But I thought the sports and social club only hired a treasurer a few months ago?'
Edward: 'They did. That's the treasurer they are looking for.'

TRANSPORT

1197. Pilot: 'What's happened to all my controls? Some idiot has daubed black and white paint all over them!'
Trainee pilot: 'But you just told me to *check* the instrument panel, sir.'

1198. The aeroplane was so old it even had an outside lavatory.

1199. On a holiday trip to Benidorm the passenger noticed the absence of any officials as the plane took off from the tarmac. Well into the flight a voice came over the speaker system: 'This is a computerised aircraft without pilot, co-pilot, stewards or stewardesses. Don't worry. There is nothing that can go wrong . . . go wrong . . . go wrong . . . go wrong . . .'

1200. The air hostess was being interviewed by her boss. 'Tell me, what would you do if you found yourself in a shallow dive?'
Air hostess: 'I'd drink up quickly and get out.'

1201. Customer: 'A return ticket, please.'
Airline reservations clerk: 'Where to, sir?'
Customer: 'Back here, please.'

1202. The light aircraft swayed to and fro above the clouds as the pilot struggled to keep control of his bird in the sky. From the look on his face it was easy to see that his struggle was coming to an end as the engine spluttered, coughed, then stopped.
It was obvious to the pilot that the aircraft would have to be evacuated and he moved inside to inform the three passengers he was carrying of his decision. Besides himself, there was a Bishop, a professor who they called Brains, and a Boy Scout.
The saddest blow of all came when the pilot informed them that although there were four people on board, there were in fact only three parachutes. Before anyone could complain and feeling that the survivors would need a leader, the pilot took one parachute and an inflatable dinghy and jumped.
Brains hurriedly grabbed for another chute because he believed that the world needed him and his knowledge, and left the Bishop and the Boy Scout behind.
The Bishop turned to the scout and, deciding to put his faith in the lord, offered him the last parachute.
After praising the Bishop for his unselfish decision the scout told him that there was no problem at all

243

because there were *two* parachutes left, not one.

'You see,' the scout told the amazed Bishop, 'Brains jumped out wearing my haversack!'

1203. Colin and Mark were enjoying a quiet country stroll when suddenly they heard a noise overhead. Looking up they saw a large aeroplane and, as they watched, the door to the cargo hold burst open and hundreds of small parts intended for a Japanese motor manufacturer fell out.

'Watch out!' cried Colin. 'It's raining Datsun cogs!'

1204. The bearded man stuck a gun in the pilot's back and hissed: 'Take me to London.'

Pilot: 'But we're supposed to be going to London anyway.'

Bearded man: 'I know. But I've been hi-jacked to Cuba twice before, so this time I'm taking no chances.'

1205. Air traffic controller: 'What is your height and position?'

Pilot: 'I'm about five feet ten inches and I'm sitting in the pilot's seat.'

1206. An old lady who was taking her time in getting off the bus called out: 'Wait a moment, driver, I'm getting on you know.' To which he replied: 'In that case, you had better sit down. I could have sworn that you were getting off.'

1207. The only reason he became a bus driver was because he wanted to tell people where to get off.

1208. I've got a two tone car – black and rust.

1209. I once bought a car designed for five people: one had to drive while the other four pushed.

1210. A careful driver is one who has just spotted a speed camera.

1211. Overheard to a chauffeur: 'James, I'm now ninety and rather bored with life, so I want to commit suicide. Kindly drive over the next cliff.'

1212. A motorist accused of a driving offence was asked: 'Why are you so sure that you were only doing fifteen miles per hour?'
'I was going to the dentist,' he replied.

1213. The car was so old and dilapidated that someone scrawled on it: 'Rust in peace'.

1214. Policeman: 'When I saw you coming round that bend I thought, "Forty-five at least".'
Woman motorist: 'Well, I always look older in this hat.'

1215. A motorist had lost his way so he enquired of a rustic who was sitting on a gate: 'Where does this road lead to?'
The reply came back: 'One way leads to my 'ome and the other way goes straight on.'

1216. Henry was trying to sell his battered old car for £900. His friend, Tom, said he would pay 10% less than the price Henry was asking for the car. But Henry was not very good at figures so he said he would think about Tom's offer. That evening, when he was in his usual bar, Henry asked the barmaid: 'If I offered you £900 less 10%, what would you take off?'
The barmaid hesitated slightly, then replied: 'Everything except my ear-rings.'

1217. A policeman in a patrol car noticed that the woman driver of a car which passed him was knitting.

He chased after her and, drawing alongside said: 'Pull over,' to which she replied: 'No, socks.'

1218. A woman was trying to get her husband to buy a new car, but he was not at all struck on the idea. 'What,' he cried, 'me buy a new car? You must think they grow on trees.'

'Of course not,' she replied. 'Don't be so silly. Everyone knows that they come from plants.'

1219. My neighbour's car is so old that it's insured against fire, theft and Viking raids.

1220. A parson was driving his car and as he slowed down to turn a corner another car came out of the turning, driven by a large woman who yelled at him the one word 'pig'.

Well, not to be outdone, the parson, who was taken by surprise, shouted in return 'cow' and then to his great consternation as he turned into the other road, there right before him was an enormous pig.

1221. A motorist whose car had broken down hailed another motorist and when he stopped, asked him if he could give him a hand.

'I'm sorry,' said the second motorist, 'but I'm a chiropodist.'

'In that case,' said the first man, 'you can give me a tow.'

1222. A policeman stopped a motorist one evening and asked him: 'Excuse me, sir, but do you realise you are driving without a rear light?'

The driver jumped out, ran to the rear of his car and gave a groan. His distress seemed so obvious that the policeman was sympathetic.

'Now, you don't have to take it so hard,' he said. 'It isn't all that serious.'

'Isn't it?' cried the motorist. 'What's happened to my caravan?'

1223. Another motorist found himself on an unfamiliar road which was narrow and had no signposts. Seeing an old man he asked if he knew where the road led to, but the old boy said he didn't know. The motorist started off again and suddenly hearing shouts, stopped and looked back to see the old chap beckoning him and indicating another old man standing near.

The motorist backed all down the narrow road and reached the two men and the first old boy said, pointing to his companion: ''E don't know, neither.'

1224. Driving instructor: 'What would you do if you were coming down that very steep hill into town and your brakes failed?'

Learner: 'Hit something cheap?'

1225. A father who was away from home all week was in the habit of taking his little daughter for a ride in his car each Sunday morning. One Sunday, however, he had a very bad cold, but rather than disappoint the little girl, her mother said that she would take her instead.

When they returned, the father asked his daughter if she had enjoyed the ride. 'Oh, yes, Daddy,' she replied. 'And do you know, we didn't see a single bastard!'

1226. I recently bought a baby car – it doesn't go anywhere without a rattle.

1227. Definitions:

Motorist – One who keeps pedestrians in good running order.

Pedestrian – A man who has found a place to park his car.

1228. *Question:* When does the pedestrian have the

right of way?

Answer: After he's placed in the ambulance.

1229. Derek: 'This car you sold me is useless.'

Car dealer: 'What's wrong with it?'

Derek: 'Within a week of me buying the thing, one of the doors fell off it, all the lights failed, the exhaust dropped off, the brakes failed, and the steering wheel came loose in my hands. I thought you said the car had only one careful owner?'

Car dealer: 'So I did. But the second owner wasn't quite so careful . . .'

1230. Our coach ground to a halt because it couldn't go any further due to the fog. A torch was pushed into my hand with instructions to find out where we were. I was fumbling about in this churchyard and came upon a gravestone. I managed to read most of it before my torch went out. On returning to the coach I told them of my escapade and they wanted to know who it was. 'He was 92,' I said. 'A bloke called Miles from London.'

1231. A cowboy had been at the saloon bar for some time and decided that it was time to go. He walked to the swing doors, looked at the hitching rail and found that his horse had gone.

'OK,' he said. 'I'm going to go back to the bar for ten minutes and if my horse ain't back, the same thing will happen here that happened in Dodge City.'

Within minutes someone came into the bar and nervously told the cowboy that his horse was back. The cowboy turned to go.

'Excuse me,' said the bartender, 'but what happened in Dodge City?'

'I had to walk home,' replied the cowboy.

1232. The lorry driver was in Eastleigh in Hampshire

248

when he slowed down his lorry and then stopped. Winding down the window of his cab he called out to a middle-aged lady: 'Excuse me, missus, but can you tell me the way to Southampton?'

'I'm sorry, I don't know,' replied the lady.

'Well do you know which direction Winchester is in?'

'No.'

'Huh!' muttered the lorry driver. 'They can't be far from here and yet you don't know which direction they're in. You don't appear to know much.'

'At least,' responded the lady, '*I* am not the one who is lost!'

1233. A lorry driver had been following a car driven by a woman somewhat erractically. At last both were halted by traffic lights and as the lorry drew alongside the car the driver saw that the woman had a large dog seated beside her. So he leaned out of his cab and said: 'If I were you, I'd let the dog drive!'

'Don't be silly,' she retorted, 'he hasn't passed his test.'

1234. A motorcyclist offered to give a friend a lift and as it was a cold day suggested that he should put on his overcoat back to front so as to avoid feeling the wind and this the passenger did and they set off. After passing over some rather bumpy ground the driver had a premonition and looking behind him saw that he had lost his passenger, so he turned round and rode back. Coming across a small crowd of people around a fallen figure he asked anxiously: 'Is he all right?'

'Well,' said one of the number, 'he was until we turned his head round the right way.'

1235. A man was lost in a dense London fog and became very alarmed when he found himself walking down a slimy alley. Suddenly he heard footsteps approaching and sighed with relief.

'Can you tell me where I am going?' he asked anxiously.

A voice replied from the darkness: 'Into the river. I've just come out.'

1236. Policeman to jay walking pedestrian: 'Here! Why are you crossing the road in this dangerous spot – can't you see there's a zebra crossing only fifty yards away?'

Pedestrian: 'Well, I hope it's having better luck than I am.'

1237. The skipper and the chief engineer of a ship were inclined to underrate each other's job, so one day they agreed to swop for a spell. All went well for a time, then the skipper called up from the engine room that he was afraid that he had messed things up.

'Don't worry,' replied the chief, 'we're aground.'

1238. An Englishwoman and her young son were travelling in a taxi in New York, USA.

As the taxi passed a particularly seedy part of the city, the small boy was fascinated by the garishly made-up ladies who were walking along the streets accosting some of the male passers by.

'What are those ladies doing?' asked the boy.

His mother blushed and said, somewhat embarrassed: 'I expect they are lost and are asking people for directions.'

The taxi driver overheard this, and said in a loud voice: 'Why don'tcha tell the boy the truth? – in udda woids they're prostitutes.'

The woman blushed even deeper red, and her son asked: 'What are p . . . p . . . pros . . . what the driver said? Are they like other women? Do they have children?'

'Of course,' replied his mother. 'That's where New York taxi drivers come from.'

1239. While travelling in a sleeping compartment in a train, the man in the top bunk was woken up by someone tapping from below. 'Hello?' he said.

'Are you awake?' asked a female voice from below.

'Yes.'

'It's terribly cold down here. I wonder if you would mind letting me have an extra blanket.'

'I've got a better idea,' replied the man. 'Let's pretend we are married.'

'That's a lovely idea!' giggled the woman.

'Right,' said the man, 'now get your own damn blanket!'

1240. Two men were sitting together in the first class compartment of a train when one of them leaned forward and said: 'Haven't I seen your face somewhere else?'

The other man paused a moment to reflect on the situation and then said: 'No, I'm sorry. But my face has always been between my ears.'

1241. I said: 'Could I have a single ticket to Jeopardy?'

He said: 'There's no such place.'

I said: 'There is. Look at this paper. It says there are a million jobs in Jeopardy!'

1242. It may interest many travellers to know that British Rail is mentioned in the Book of Genesis. It states that God created every creeping thing.

1243. Three men came to a railway platform and, finding that there was some time to wait until the train was due, went into the buffet for a drink, or to be precise, a succession of drinks. Suddenly the train came roaring into the station and the three men burst out of the buffet and two of them clambered into a carriage, being helped in with plenty of shoving by the third man.

The train departed and then the third man collapsed on to a platform seat with helpless laughter. A porter approached him and asked if there was anything the matter and the man replied: 'Did you see those two men who went off on that train?' The porter nodded and the man then said: 'Well, they came to see *me* off!'

1244. A traveller in a train on a slow surburban line noticed that a fellow passenger alighted from the carriage each time that the train stopped and hurried off to the booking office, returning in time for the train to start off again. Thinking that perhaps there was some particular reason for this, the traveller asked his companion, an elderly man, if there was anything the matter and if he could be of assistance.

'Oh, no,' the man replied. 'You see, my doctor tells me that I've a weak heart and as I'm liable to drop dead at any moment, I'm only booking from station to station.'

1245. A train which had been proceeding along very slowly at last came to a halt miles from anywhere, so it seemed. The passengers were all peering out of the windows when the guard was observed walking along the track by the side of the train. This gave one facetious passenger his chance: 'Guard,' he called out, 'can I get out and pick some flowers?'

'What do you mean?' the guard replied. 'There aren't any flowers here.'

'Oh, I've got a packet of seeds,' came the reply.

1246. A Frenchman who was visiting Ireland entered a compartment of a train and in the carriage were two Irishmen who were commercial travellers. One of these said to the other: 'And where have ye been lately?'

'Sure,' came the reply, 'and haven't I been to Kilmary and now I'm off to Kilpatrick. And what about yerself?'

The first replied: 'I've been to Kilkenny and to Kilmichael and now I'm off to Kilmore.'

The Frenchman listened in amazement. 'Murdering scoundrels!' he thought and got out at the next station.

1247. It was announced today that British Rail are to place boards over the bottom of the lavatory doors at Waterloo Station. A spokesman said this was to prevent limbo dancers from getting in free.

1248. An American visitor to England was a passenger in a train and, striking up a conversation with an Englishman who was in his compartment said: 'Do you know that you can board a train in Texas, and after travelling for 24 hours you'd still be in Texas?'

The Englishman replied: 'Yes, I know. We have trains like that in this country.'

1249. The skipper of a tramp steamer was a stickler for the facts. So, when the mate came aboard rather the worse for liquor one evening, he duly entered in the log: 'Mate drunk today', explaining that it was true and that he had to record it.

When it was the mate's turn to make the day's entries in the log, the skipper was horrified to read: 'Captain sober today.'

'What does this mean?' he asked.

'Well,' said the mate, 'it was true and I had to enter it.'

1250. A customs officer at Kennedy Airport, New York, opened the suitcase of a beautiful young girl from England and discovered six pairs of very brief panties. He took them out of the case for further inspection (in the vain hope of finding some concealed drugs) and found that the panties were each labelled with one day of the week, from Monday to Saturday.

'And on Sunday?' he inquired.

The girl blushed.

The next person to be inspected by the customs officer was an enormously fat woman from Montreal, and the customs officer took out twelve pairs of giant-size bloomers from her suitcase. Before he could say anything, the Montreal lady smirked, patted his arm playfully and said: 'January, February, March, April, May . . .'